Also by Bob Cullen

(Fiction)

Soviet Sources
Cover Story
Dispatch from a Cold Country
Heirs of the Fire

(Nonfiction)

Twilight of Empire
The Killer Department

(Collaborating with Dr. Bob Rotella)

Golf Is Not a Game of Perfect
Golf Is a Game of Confidence
The Golf of Your Dreams
Life Is Not a Game of Perfect

Why Golf?

The Mystery of the Game Revisited

Bob Cullen

SIMON & SCHUSTER

NEW YORK LONDON TORONTO SYDNEY SINGAPORE

SIMON & SCHUSTER
Rockefeller Center
1230 Avenue of the Americas
New York, NY 10020

Designed by O'Lanso Gabbidon
Manufactured in the United States of America

10 9 8 7 6 5 4 3 2 1

Library of Congress Cataloging-In-Publication Data

ISBN 0-7432-4247-5

For information regarding the special discounts for bulk purchases, please contact Simon
& Schuster Special Sales at 1-800-456-6798 or business@simonandschuster.com

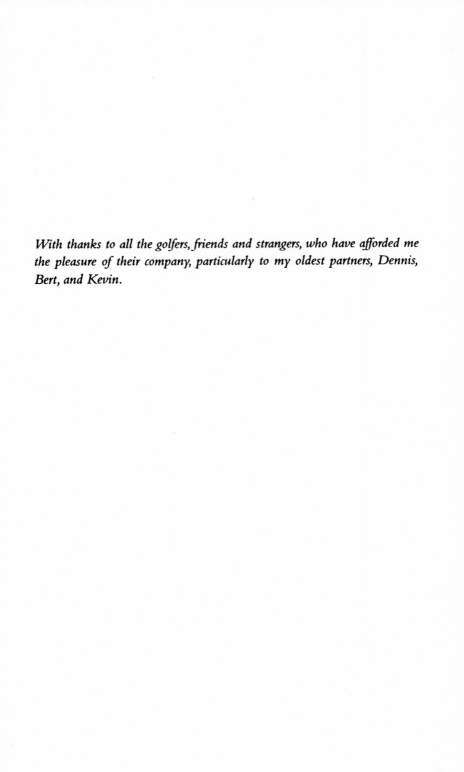

With thanks to all the golfers, friends and strangers, who have afforded me the pleasure of their company, particularly to my oldest partners, Dennis, Bert, and Kevin.

Contents

Why Golf?

Introduction

This book is an extended response to a question, a question posed to me several years ago by an old friend named Alex Beam, who writes a column for *The Boston Globe.* Alex had just won a Knight Fellowship, which is one of the plummiest things a reporter can win. Knight Fellows get to hang out for a year at Stanford University, reading what they want to read, attending classes when they want to go. A Knight Fellowship is a second chance at being a college student, except that there are no grades and it comes to people at a time in life when they are smart enough to appreciate the privilege. Some Knight Fellows work assiduously on acquiring knowledge. Some work assiduously on their tans. Most work on a combination of the two.

I had been a Knight Fellow years before, and Alex asked me how I would recommend he spend his time. For a few minutes I gave him the sorts of pieties that he and I had both used to persuade the program to let us in. I told him about the opportunity to explore new intellectual horizons, to learn about drama and classical music. I told him about the brilliant faculty and the books I'd read. Then I told him the truth.

"Stanford has a wonderful golf course," I said. "You can play whenever you want, for the student green fee. It's a great deal."

In fact, Stanford had been where I rediscovered golf. I had arrived in September of my fellowship year without clubs, having spent the decade of my twenties with neither the funds nor the inclination to pursue the game. Golf slipped gradually, almost surreptitiously into my life that year. In December I needed to pass some time during Christmas break while my wife, Ann, finished work on a book. I bought a driver, a five-iron, and a putter at a secondhand sporting goods store. By March I had a full, if mismatched, set of secondhand clubs and I was arranging my class schedule to leave big blocks of time free in the afternoon. By May I was making pilgrimages to Pebble Beach.

Alex was not impressed. "Why," he asked me, his voice tinged with scorn, "would an intelligent person play golf?"

Perhaps this should not have surprised me. Alex and I had known each other in Moscow, where I was stationed after Stanford. In those pre-*glasnost* years, Russians did not play golf. The land was covered with ice and snow for half the year, and the Soviets weren't very good at growing things, whether grass or wheat, during the other half. Besides, golf was seen by the Communist Party as a capitalist sport. It was not in the Olympics, so there was no propaganda value in developing golfers. Thus there were no golf courses in the Soviet Union. Alex and I and the rest of the Moscow press corps had contented ourselves with pastimes that included cross-country skiing, platform tennis on the court behind the American ambassador's house, and a peculiar, slightly clownish derivative of hockey played in sneakers on ice, called broomball. We had never had occasion to discuss golf.

But there it was. He disdained the game.

For once I had a glib rejoinder.

"Why don't you ask John Updike?" I said.

Updike, as it happens, likes golf. We both knew he had just published a collection of his golf writing. And both Alex and I had, as novelists, labored in the undergrowth at the foot of the mountain on which Updike sits. My citing Updike's good opinion of the game was the rough equivalent of a Soviet politician citing Lenin back in our Moscow days. It stifled argument.

"Touché," Alex said.

But after the conversation ended, Alex's question continued to bother me. Certainly there were intelligent people devoted to golf. But that didn't answer the question. Why were they devoted to it?

To put it more personally, why was I so devoted to it? In the years following my return from Moscow, golf's place in my life had grown from pastime to hobby to passion. In the preceding couple of years, it had become part of my profession as well. I had helped Dr. Bob Rotella to write a couple of successful books on the psychology of the game, *Golf Is Not a Game of Perfect* and *Golf Is a Game of Confidence*. But I had thought very little about why the game had such a growing hold on me.

The golf literature I had accumulated in my work did not, for the most part, address the question. There were plenty of books about how to play the game. There were lots of works about the great players and their exploits. But I had encountered only one book that addressed the question Alex had posed.

This was a small volume called *The Mystery of Golf,* by Arnold Haultain. Written in 1908, it was first published in a very small edition of several hundred copies. Those sold out, and a larger edition was published two years later. Over the years the book had enjoyed a durable popularity among golfers. It was still in print in various editions nearly nine decades after its first appearance.

From the book, and from a trip to the Library of Congress, I learned a few things about the author. Haultain was born in India in 1857 and died in England in 1941. As a young man, he migrated to Canada, and at the turn of the century, he was working as the personal secretary to one of the leading intellectuals of the period, Goldwin Smith. Smith, a transplanted English historian, taught at both Cornell and the University of Toronto.

Haultain published a number of books, but none of the

others were as perspicacious or successful as *The Mystery of Golf*. He wrote *Two Walks in Canada* about a hiking tour of parts of his adopted country, in which he assured his readers that Quebec's French-speaking population had happily accepted union with anglophone Canada. He penned something called *Hints for Lovers,* which must have seemed insipid even to the Edwardians. It is full of statements like "A woman never brings pure reason to bear on her actions. She acts by sentiment."

But when it came to golf, Haultain got the question right. "Will someone please tell us," he wrote, "wherein lies the extraordinary fascination of golf?"

He was, he wrote, a recent convert to the game, suggesting that he had taken it up in his forties. He displayed the zeal of the convert, of a man who had chosen his faith rather than having it bestowed upon him.

"I have just come home from my club," he recounted. "We played till we could not see the flag. The caddies were sent ahead to find the balls by the thud of their fall. And a large, low moon threw whispering shadows on the dew-wet grass ere we trode the home green. At dinner, the talk was of golf, and for three mortal hours after dinner, the talk was of golf. Yet the talkers were neither idiots, fools or monomaniacs. [They were] trying to probe or elucidate the profundities and complexities of this so-called 'game.' "

From such conversations Haultain wove a book. As the employee of a leading intellectual, he was at least acquainted with the latest thinking of his time in human psychology and biology. He used what he knew to construct some hypotheses, hypotheses that have stood the passage of nine decades rather well. He recognized, for instance, that the game's fascination rested much less on its physical challenges than on the way it engages the mind.

But it seemed to me that it might well be time to revisit the question. We know quite a bit more about the human psyche now than we knew in 1908. Or, at least, a large number of research scientists have made a living over that time conducting experiments on human beings and publishing the results. It might be interesting to apply what they learned to golf and see what insights it produced.

So for several years I kept Alex Beam's question in mind during my own play and in my reporting forays into the world of golf. As a golf journalist, I am a dilettante. I cover no tournaments, write no stories on tight deadlines, and I don't know a lot of what most golf journalists learned long ago. But my work did allow me the freedom to consider the question of why while others answered who, what, when, and where. This did not strike me as an unmitigated disadvantage.

Why the Blind Baby Smiled

Probably ninety percent of human outdoor games consist in the propulsion of a spheroid or spheroidal object to a certain spot.

—Haultain

The essence of golf is simple. The player has a ball. It lies at point A. Using a club, he tries to move it to point B.

It is an essentially useless endeavor. The ball does the player no more good at point B than it did at point A. There is no evident reason why moving it there should make him happy.

Yet there is no doubt that it does. Before there were courses and rules, scores and tournaments, before there was even a game called golf, there was the pleasure to be found in this simple act.

The joy of whacking something is the common thread in the childhood histories of virtually all the great golfers. Harry Vardon recounted how he and his friends on the Isle of Jersey built clubs to smack a white marble called a taw over the commons of the village of Grouville in 1877. Bobby Jones recalled how, at the age of five, he and a friend would while away summer days on the roadway in front of his Atlanta house, hitting a ball into a ditch with a sawed-off cleek given him by a member of the East Lake Country Club. Sam Snead made himself a club with a buggy whip for a shaft and a head fashioned from a knot in a tree branch. He happily banged rocks around the hills and pastures of Ashwood, Virginia, with this club until one Sunday morning when he happened to hit one through the window of the local Baptist church. Arnold Palmer, in his autobiography, recalls how his father gave him a club when he was three years old, taught him to grip it, and gave him a simple lesson: "Hit it hard, boy. Go find it and hit it again." This Palmer did, with great delight. He is still doing it, with evident zest, nearly seven decades later. In fact, the pleasure he finds in following his father's instruction could well be the reason he has played the game as well as he has for as long as he has.

Still, why should this be so?

I play golf once in a while with a psychiatrist named Joe Silvio. We met at a party given by a mutual friend several years ago. When I mentioned that I played, it was like mentioning that I knew an old flame he hadn't seen since college. His face lit up with a mixture of fondness, nostalgia, and hope. "Golf was the joy of my youth," he said.

I couldn't help but invite him to play.

Joe showed up for our game with a nervous smile on his bearded face and a set of clubs in an old leather bag. The irons were rusty. The driver was an old steel-shafted persimmon, so clearly a product of the fifties that it almost had tail fins. But when he hit a few range balls to loosen up, it was clear that he'd once played well. He had the fundamentals—good posture at address, a full turn. His timing showed the effects of a few decades of rust. Some of his shots came off the hosel and some off the toe. They banged against the fence on the side of the range.

But it was one of those rare, soft summer days without heat or humidity, a day of blue skies and scattered, high clouds, the kind of July day that once in a while gets lost in Canada and wanders down to Maryland before regaining its bearings. No matter what the ball did, Joe was happy to be there.

"I'm not expecting much today," he said, as much to himself as to me.

He grounded his drive off the first tee. Mine wasn't much better—into the rough on the left side of the fairway. I didn't care. I was having too much fun watching Joe rediscover the game. He didn't care how many strokes he took. He was enjoying the sensation of hitting a golf ball.

"Golf was a big factor in my boyhood," he said as we walked down the first hole.

He grew up, he told me, in Elizabeth, New Jersey. Elizabeth, as anyone who drives down the New Jersey Turnpike knows, is the place where New York stores its oil, in vast tank farms that smell of benzine. It's where freighters unload their cargoes. It's not a place generally associated with golf.

"My father was an oil worker for Esso," he said. "But when I was a kid I got a job as a caddie at a public course called Galloping Hill, near the Garden State Parkway. After a while there, I graduated to a private club called Suburban Country Club. I worked on the weekends and in the summer. I played on Mondays."

Working at a golf club, he remembered, had paid him more than money. It had given him a chance to meet and talk with doctors, lawyers, engineers—people he would not necessarily have encountered in Elizabeth. Slowly he realized that he was able to handle himself in their company, that they were no smarter than he was. He credited this experience with helping him decide to become a doctor. He applied for a scholarship available to the children of Esso employees and got it. He went to Cornell.

But the price of this upward mobility, it seemed, was golf. He married and started a private psychiatric practice. He and his wife had children. He decided he couldn't spare the time for activities that did not involve them. So the clubs got old in a corner of the garage.

By the time we made the turn, Joe's swing was slowly coming back. He was making bogeys and double bogeys. I was playing my usual game, which was perhaps a stroke per hole better. We weren't competing. He wasn't even keeping score.

The conversation flitted from golf to psychology and back again. We talked about criminal madness and a book I'd written about a Russian serial killer. We talked about the slice and what caused it. He told me how he'd come to rely less and less on Freudian theories over the years, finding that they were useful in explaining aggressive behavior but not very helpful in curing other illnesses.

I was thinking about my conversation with Alex Beam, so as we putted out on the twelfth hole, I asked him what Freud might have said about why people play golf.

"Freud probably would have explained it in terms of some kind of penis symbolism," he said.

The thirteenth at my course is a par three, one hundred and ninety-five yards. Joe hit his best shot of the day there, a three-iron that drew sweetly into the middle of the green. It was a reminder of the skills he'd once had and a promise that he might yet recapture them.

More than that, it was a reminder of the pleasure of the well-struck ball. I was not sure why hitting a golf ball well feels so good. There is, I knew, a pleasing sense of grace and rhythm that accompanies the swing on good shots. There's a strong, solid feeling that flows from the center of the club-face, through the shaft, into the hands, and up to the brain when a ball is hit properly. That's why, I suppose, the center of the clubface is called the sweet spot. Then there's the sight of the ball arcing against the sky and the trees, tracking toward its target. I am not one of those players who hits a good drive and reaches down to find and retrieve the used tee before the ball lands. When I catch one well, I savor every second of the ball's flight.

Joe, I could see, felt the same way. He watched his ball roll to a stop with a pleased smile on his face.

"I must've pulled that one out of my deep subconscious," he grinned.

Actually, Joe told me as we walked toward the green, Freud was considered badly outdated as a theorist on the sources of human pleasure. He had postulated a couple of instinctive drives—a sexual drive, an aggressive drive. More recent research had suggested a model of the psyche that featured five instincts, though now they were called, with the academic tendency toward verbiage inflation, "motivational systems."

"Golf is probably related to the exploratory-assertive motivational system," he said.

I chipped onto the green and felt unusually conscious of the sensory pleasure the shot gave me. It was a good chip, hit with a seven-iron from a clean lie. I caught the ball just before the clubhead reached the bottom of its arc, making the kind of contact that presses the ball down toward the ground for a millisecond before it reacts to the loft of the clubface and gets airborne, like a watermelon seed squeezed from between pursed lips. The ball hit the green a few feet from the collar and bounced the way a ball struck with backspin bounces—alertly, like a dog on a leash sniffing for a scent. Then it rolled smartly toward the hole, taking the expected break and dying inches from the cup for a tap-in par. I enjoyed the shot, enjoyed the feeling of controlling the ball.

Joe missed his birdie putt, but he was happy to take a par during this introductory round.

"What's the exploratory-assertive motivational system?" I asked him as we headed for the fourteenth tee.

He told me the story of the blind baby who smiled.

It seems that a psychiatrist was working with an infant

born blind. At the age of eight weeks, the baby had never smiled, something that infants blessed with eyesight do at roughly the age of four weeks. But how could a blind infant be expected to smile? He could not see his mother's smiling face.

The doctors experimented with different sounds in their efforts to stimulate the baby. They introduced small bells into the area around his cradle. The sound of the bells, though, did not make the baby smile—not at first.

The doctors rigged an apparatus that allowed the infant to control the sound of the bells by kicking his legs. Very quickly, the baby got the hang of it. He kicked. He heard a bell ring. He kicked again. The bell rang again.

The baby smiled. He smiled every time his kicking produced the bell sound, even though the sound of the bells had never caused him to smile when it was just a random occurrence in his environment.

What pleased the infant, then, was not the sound of the bell, per se. It was causing the sound of the bell. He smiled because he had discovered he could make something happen around him. He could manipulate his environment.

That, Joe told me, was one of the experimental bases for the theory of the exploratory-assertive motivational system. Making something happen in the environment around them gives human beings a sense of competence. That, in turn, gives them pleasure. A baby will indefatigably use his arms and legs to push the pieces of a mobile hanging above his crib, simply for the pleasure of seeing them move in response to his actions. A golfer will happily spend hours on the practice range hitting seven-irons to a flag in the ground one hundred and fifty yards away. Both the baby and the golfer are impelled by the same instinct.

Joe's explanation reminded me of something I had recently observed far from a golf course. It was the early stages of a new sport called punkin' chunkin'. Punkin' chunkin', in the light of Joe's explanation, seemed like a very basic manifestation of the exploratory-assertive motivational system.

It began a few years ago in the fields around Lewes, Delaware, when some farmers had to dispose of their unsold pumpkins after Halloween. Someone suggested a contest to build devices that would heave the pumpkins across a field, where they splattered in a very satisfactory way. Punkin' chunkin' was born.

Punkin' chunkin' touched something within the psyches of the people of the Delmarva Peninsula. Within a few years the informal little contest had grown to a major spectacle. The simple early catapults used to heave the pumpkins evolved rapidly until there were several classes of implements. In the unlimited class the pumpkin heavers turned into launchers the size and length of water mains, powered by gas or compressed air, mounted on heavy trucks with names like the Destroyer. The distance the pumpkins traveled edged past half a mile. A little Presbyterian church at the far end of the field had to be boarded up for protection during the contest.

The town of Lewes organized punkin' chunkin' into a late autumn festival. Fences were erected and tickets were sold. Budweiser became a corporate sponsor. And thousands of spectators showed up each November to watch people heave pumpkins across a plowed field, to see the vegetable arc against the sky and splatter against the ground. It was entertainment at its most elemental.

"Yeah, Joe," I said. "That sounds plausible."

Heaving pumpkins. Hitting baseballs. Throwing a basketball through a hoop. Playing golf. They all stemmed from the same instinct.

We were playing the seventeenth hole, a short par five. I tried to crank out a long drive. As is usual in such cases, I threw off my rhythm and cut the ball, pushing it into the right rough, in a spot from which I would have no chance to reach the green in two.

"Still, I'm not sure Freud wouldn't have been right in equating the urge to hit a golf ball with some kind of symbol of virility," I said to Joe as we walked after our balls. "Isn't that why people love to see John Daly or Tiger Woods more than Corey Pavin or Lee Janzen, even though Pavin and Janzen have won U.S. Opens and Woods and Daly haven't? They're the big studs because they hit it three hundred yards."

Joe shrugged, wordlessly expressing his opinion of Freud. "I think you'll find that Freud was best suited to his own era, when a lot of things were more repressed," he said.

As if to demonstrate how the long drive was overrated, I got onto the green in a regulation three strokes and missed a short birdie putt. It was the putting, more than the length of the tee shot, that determined the score.

Joe's old leather bag gave out as we played the last hole. He picked it up and the strap pulled away from the body of the bag. He carried it down the last fairway with the strap slung over his shoulder and clenched in his right hand, the way boys carried their schoolbooks when Freud's theories were new and in fashion.

He was far from discouraged. "I've got to get a new bag and maybe some clubs," he said. "Should I buy new or used?"

I suggested that Joe get back into the game the way I had years before at Stanford. I told him he should go to a used sporting goods store and buy some secondhand clubs to use until he could better determine the state of both his swing and his interest. I recommended a lightweight nylon bag with a pop-up stand; Joe, with commendable instincts, had already decided that he wanted to avoid golf carts whenever possible and tote his own clubs.

Joe had a suggestion for me. "You should go see Joe Lichtenberg," he said. Lichtenberg was a psychiatrist, a professor at the Georgetown University School of Medicine. He had written a book, *Psychoanalysis and Motivation,* that summarized the research that developed the model of five motivational systems.

I found a copy and read it. The exploratory-assertive motivational system turned out to be one of those scientific terms of art that conceal more than they illuminate, at least for those not immersed every day in the jargon of the trade. Essentially, it means that if you give a human being an opportunity, he will explore his environment and try to make things happen in it. It's another way of saying we're active and curious. It's another way of saying we like to be in control of our surroundings. It's another way of saying we like to be good at exerting this control.

It also turned out that in experimenting with these tendencies, it was remarkably easy to get infants to display the traits that make golfers like to hit golf balls.

For instance, if you take four-month-olds and expose them to five-second bursts of multicolored light, you will get their attention for a while. But, being infants, the babies will soon get bored. They will stop turning toward the source of the multicolored light.

If, however, you rig the display so that the infants can turn it on by turning their heads from side to side three times, their interest picks up dramatically. The infants will shake their heads so steadily they resemble Soviet arms control negotiators in the bad old days of the Brezhnev regime. They *love* the idea that something they do with their bodies affects something in their environment.

Dr. Lichtenberg, of course, was not the first to notice the tendency. Even Freud wrote of the way his grandson, at eighteen months, liked to throw small objects out of sight and then hunt for them. He would do this over and over again, making them disappear and reappear in his world.

Toymakers have known about it for generations. Think of the pleasure children get from their hammers and Peg-Boards, toys that consist of nothing more than an opportunity to wield a sort of club and bang a peg so that it protrudes from one side of the board rather than the other. The child bangs all the pegs through to one side, then happily turns the board over and bangs them through to the other.

Dr. Lichtenberg's role was not to discover this trait. He assimilated the experimental results of many researchers and interpreted them to produce his model of the psyche.

The doctor, as it happened, lived not far from me. I called him up and asked for an appointment. He sounded politely skeptical of my explanation—that I had read his book and wanted to ask him some questions about his theories and the light they might shed on the pleasures of golf. No doubt he had found that disturbed patients can present their cases in eccentric ways. I made a point of carrying a notebook when I went to his office. I kept it clutched in my hand as I made my way through the little maze of doors and corridors he had erected to protect his patients' privacy as they came and went.

Dr. Lichtenberg was a short, wiry man with graying hair. He dressed soberly in a white shirt, a tie, a conservative blue suit, and sensible shoes in black leather. He projected dispassionate rationality. He did not, he told me, play golf. He sailed. He played tennis. He took long, regular swims. While he swam he mentally composed paragraphs for his books.

He had been thinking about my query, he went on, and had some ideas. He agreed with Joe Silvio that the exploratory-assertive motivational system was fundamental to the pleasures of golf. But it was not the only factor. He thought all five of the human motivational systems played a role.

So we sat down—I chose an armchair facing him and kept a measured distance from the couch along the far wall. Dr. Lichtenberg shared his thoughts as he might if lecturing a small group of medical students.

The first instinct, he said, is the regulation of our bodies. We are born wanting to eat and sleep, of course. But we also want to control our movement. Babies in the womb, for instance, know how to bring their hands to their mouths to suck their fingers. Immediately after birth, they've lost this ability. It's because moving body parts through the air is different from moving them through the fluid environment of the uterus. Infants seem to resent this loss of control. In the first days of life, they struggle to remaster the skill. At first they push their hands past their mouths. In about ten days, though, they learn. It gives them satisfaction to move their hands to their mouths and suck.

In another decade or two, the same instinct might be prompting those infants to master ballet or tennis or golf. All three are disciplines that call for mastery of complex movements. When we master such movements, when they flow as if by instinct, we have a word that describes what we have done: graceful. It implies that a higher power has helped us control our bodies.

It is, I suppose, the search for that state of grace that impels dancers and golfers to practice. Or, as Lichtenberg explained it, "We work to get the brain to run the musculature in a very particular way. There's a pleasure that comes when it's beautifully coordinated."

The second general instinct in Dr. Lichtenberg's model of the psyche was what he called the "attachment-affiliation system." To put it less clinically, we all want to love and be loved. We all want to have friends.

Golf, Lichtenberg said, struck him as a peculiarly good sport for friendship. As a tennis player, he had noted that golf, unlike most sports, did not require the division of the players into two sides. Tennis did so by means of a net. In football the teams defended opposite ends of a field. Other sports had goals or baskets. They all came down to skins against shirts, home versus away, us against them. You can't have a game without having a winner and a loser.

But golf, as Joe Silvio and I had rediscovered, lends itself to a completely noncompetitive, friendly approach. I could think of hundreds of pleasant rounds in the company of both friends and total strangers with no match on, nothing at stake. We simply enjoyed the game together.

In fact, golf is a sport that has to be slightly modified if the players want to make it more competitive, want to have a winner and a loser. That's why a lot of golfers normally bet a few dollars at the start of a round. It's why the game maintains an elaborate handicap system. It's why clubs have tournaments. The game is like a sports car. You can soup it up and race it, but it's also great for relaxed cruising on a sunny day.

Dr. Lichtenberg kept ticking off the instincts that made golf attractive. The third, he thought, was the goal of sensual pleasure, the esthetic instinct. This instinct makes some of us love Impressionist paintings. It also, he thought, makes golfers love golf courses. "Golf has created a setting that's highly pleasurable. People gravitate toward the course for this reason," he said. "It allows us to combine the sensual appreciation of art with the playful, exploratory, adventurous side of our personalities."

The fourth instinct was a negative one, he said. Human beings are wired to react adversely to certain things—foul tastes, foul deeds. We respond with anger, fear, disdain, contempt, sarcasm, shame, or sadness—perhaps a combination of several. This instinct, restrained to moderate levels, helps people resolve conflicts and avoid danger. Unchecked, of course, it can be the source of terrible unhappiness.

I smiled. That, I told him, was something good golfers knew. I remembered Sam Snead saying he tried never to be more than "sensibly irritated" at anything that happened on the golf course.

Finally, Dr. Lichtenberg concluded, there was the exploratory-assertive instinct, the one Joe Silvio had cited to me. It is the instinct behind both work and play.

The spontaneous play of children and infants, he said, follows a few general patterns. They seek stimulation and contact with the environment. They like activity to require a degree of persistence. Finally, kids at play want some risk, some tension.

"One's interest in efficacy has to be stimulated, or the play becomes boring" is the way Dr. Lichtenberg put it.

But kids don't want the tension in their play to be so great as to frighten them, Dr. Lichtenberg went on. A frisson of tension pleases us; panic does not. Thus, for example, most boys will walk on top of a six-foot fence, but not on a wire a hundred feet off the ground. Thus, most people bet two dollars a side, not their houses, when they play golf.

Kids also appreciate novelty and variety in their play, the doctor noted. They're delighted by slight variations in their games—much as golfers delight in new courses and new holes.

Kids at play enjoy developing competence, whether it be with a yo-yo, a top, or a club and a ball. That's one reason successful societies encourage children to play. The urge to develop competence is thought to spill over into their work and studies.

Or, if they're fortunate, into golf, I thought.

Yet another golf-related feature of the exploratory-assertive system, Dr. Lichtenberg went on, was something called the Ziegarnik Effect.

"The Ziegarnik Effect?" I asked.

The Ziegarnik Effect, he replied, is the name given to a tendency that emerged in a series of experiments regarding complex tasks. Subjects were given a job like adding seven rows of numbers. Then the researcher stopped them in the middle of doing this job and asked them to do something else. When this second chore was completed, the researcher gave the subjects a choice of activities. Most subjects chose to go back to the seven rows of numbers and finish adding them up. "People want to keep going," Dr. Lichtenberg said. "They want to finish what they've started."

"Like the eighteen holes of a golf course?" I asked.

He nodded.

The Ziegarnik Effect, he said, helps explain the satisfaction of the structure of the game. Golf gives us eighteen separate tasks and eighteen satisfying moments of completion before it rewards us with the grand satisfaction of completing the course. It would be, after all, possible to lay out a seven-thousand-yard course with one tee and one hole. No one does so. It would reduce the pleasure of the game.

Dr. Lichtenberg put down his notes. He had covered everything, he said politely, and my fifty minutes were almost up. He had a patient due shortly. Did I have any brief questions?

Well, I said, he had shed a lot of light on the pleasures of the game. Obviously, golf stimulates some parts of the brain that are wired to give us enjoyment. His model of the psyche did not, of course, explain completely why golf was more addictive than, say, competitive archery. But it helped.

I did have one question. Why, if he thought golf would be so well suited to the pleasure centers of the psyche, did he not play himself?

Dr. Lichtenberg responded with the wry smile of a man who long ago sorted through the messy passions of life and made strictly rational choices about which ones he would indulge.

"The learning curve is too steep," he said. "I never felt I wanted to take the time to learn."

Clipped Grasslands

*It would be interesting to dive into the primaeval origin of games
and to discuss whether the first distinct differentiation of the man
from the ape consisted not in the ability to throw a stone and wield
a bough.*

—Haultain

D
r. Lichtenberg's model of the psyche shed some light
on golf's appeal. But it didn't fully explain why some
people find golf more instinctively absorbing than
punkin' chunkin' or basketball. And it didn't explain why
those instincts exist.

Haultain had sensed that the answer to those questions
lay in human prehistory. But in his era, at the turn of the
century, the study of prehistory had almost been aborted before it began. Charles Darwin had published *The Origin of
Species* in 1859. Unfortunately, Darwin's theory of evolution
through natural selection was quickly hijacked by the Social
Darwinists, who used it, crudely and incorrectly, to rational-
ize the gulf between rich and poor in the age of the robber
barons. By the time Haultain got around to writing *The
Mystery of Golf,* Darwinism was tainted, in much the way

that, say, the Heaven's Gate cult tainted the work of as-
tronomers who seriously pursue the possibility of extrater-
restrial life.

Only in the past thirty years or so has Darwinism managed
to rehabilitate itself as a tool for understanding the nature of
contemporary human beings. A new discipline, evolutionary
psychology, has emerged. It studies the way that evolution has
made our minds and behavior the way they are.

I know this not because I keep up with the latest develop-
ments in the life sciences—I don't. I know it because of a
book written by an occasional golfing partner, Bob Wright.
His book *The Moral Animal* is both an interpretive biography
of Darwin and an exegesis of how the theory of evolution has
itself evolved in the past three decades. I wanted to know
more about golf and what Haultain had called "the primaeval
origin." So I reread the book and called Bob for a game. We
agreed to meet at a golf course he frequents, in Rock Creek
Park.

Rock Creek Park Golf Course sits about three miles north
of the White House, in the middle of a park that runs like a
green spine down the center of the District of Columbia.
Despite its proximity to the seat of power, there is no record
that any president has ever played it. Chief executives tend to
prefer private courses out in the suburbs.

It's their loss. Rock Creek is honest, muni golf, fifteen dollars a round, par 68, weedy fairways, shaggy greens, no frills,
and a bunch of sharks hanging out on the practice green, playing complicated games for a quarter a putt. It's the sort of place
where you don't worry first about your opening tee shot. You
worry first about finding a place on the hardpan tee soft
enough so you can push the peg into the ground. I liked it.

Bob was dressed in his usual golf apparel, topped by a ma-
roon cap from Slate, the on-line magazine that publishes
some of his articles. His eyeglasses bespoke many more hours
spent in libraries than on golf courses. He is one of those
people who's too dedicated to his work to play as much golf

as he'd like. He grew up as a military brat and learned the game on military courses like the Presidio in San Francisco. His opportunities to play have been sporadic since then. "Whenever I get a chance to play much, I fall in love with it," he once told me. But then, like a married man who gives up an affair for the sake of the family, he returns to his desk for months on end. Lately, he said, he'd been giving some thought to becoming a more frequent player. He thought that with a lesson or two and some work on his short game, he could start to play consistently in the 90s.

He took an iron off the first tee. I found a clump of chickweed into which I could press my tee and hit driver. Every starting hole should be so accommodating. Number one at Rock Creek is a two-hundred-and-ninety-four-yard par four with a fairway as wide as a football field. This being late summer, and the course having no irrigation system, that fairway was baked to a consistency only slightly softer than the pavement on Sixteenth Street, behind our backs. My ball rolled like a marble on a kitchen floor, not stopping until it was a chip shot away from the green. My chip was stiff, and I marked down a three as we walked toward the second tee.

Starting off with a birdie always makes me feel a little animalish, even if it's at Rock Creek Park. I found myself thinking of prehistoric environments and natural selection.

The theory behind evolutionary psychology holds that our genes influence more than just the color of our eyes and the shape of our noses—our physical beings. They also influence our behavior and emotions. (Culture and upbringing also influence behavior, to be sure. But they are overlaid on a genetic framework that neither parents nor society controls.) People may be bold or timid, smart or stupid, hotheaded or cool-tempered in varying situations in part because of genes passed along to them by preceding generations.

The process of passing genes from one generation to the next assures that the traits that give advantages in the competition to survive and reproduce will come to dominate in the overall population. The classic, and overdrawn, example of how this works is the evolutionary psychologist's explanation for male promiscuity. The theory suggests that in prehistoric times there might have been men with a tendency toward monogamous fidelity and men with a tendency to fool around. All other things being equal, the promiscuous men would impregnate more women and pass their genetic tendency toward promiscuity on to more members of the next generation. The third generation would have yet more males with a tendency to promiscuity. And so on, until the general population was dominated by promiscuous males.

It is not hard to imagine how natural selection might have favored prehumans with a healthy genetic dose of the traits Dr. Lichtenberg packaged under the title "exploratory-assertive motivational system." Very suggestive evidence comes from recent observations of wild chimpanzee colonies in Africa, most notably by Jane Goodall.

Chimpanzees are man's closest relatives. And the environments in which they live are probably very similar to the environments in which the human gene pool began to take shape—a dense forest in Africa, populated by clusters of perhaps several dozen individuals. (The vexatious state of modern humanity is due in some part to the fact that we are trying to live in an atomized, postindustrial world with bodies wired to survive and reproduce within a small, tightly knit group inhabiting a wilderness environment. Some one hundred thousand to two hundred thousand generations stand between modern *Homo sapiens* and the hominid called *Australopithecus,* which walked upright and had an apelike brain. The vast majority—perhaps ninety-nine percent—of those generations lived in conditions much closer to those of chimps than to those of, say, modern Manhattan.)

When Goodall began living among and observing chimps in the Gombe Stream Reserve of Tanzania in 1960, her presence, of course, changed the chimps' environment. Among other things, she established a camp and used a kerosene stove. That meant that in the vicinity of the camp there were soon empty four-gallon kerosene cans.

Many of the chimps instinctively shied away from Goodall and her camp. But some were more curious, more interested in exploring, more eager to see how they could assert themselves in the changed environment they encountered. One of the latter group was a male chimp Goodall named Mike.

Mike discovered that he could make an especially fierce and noisy display by banging two empty kerosene cans together. It happens that displays of ferocity are among the primary tactics male chimps use in their competition to achieve the status of alpha, or dominant, male in their colony. Mastery of the kerosene cans gave Mike an immediate advantage in this competition. He took to charging at the other males in the colony, banging his cans together, creating a terrible ruckus. He intimidated them. As a result, Mike rose quickly from the bottom of the male hierarchy to the top. He became alpha male.

Since one of the perks of alphahood is enhanced access to fertile females in the colony, it's not hard to see how the next generation of chimps would have more of Mike's tendency to be curious, to explore, to whack things. Extrapolating from there, it's not hard to see how a significant percentage of today's human population might be endowed with the genes for Lichtenberg's exploratory-assertive motivational system—and how they might instinctively enjoy playing golf.

But that, I thought, was not all that evolutionary psychology could teach about the origins of the instinctive pleasures of golf. For one thing, it did not explain why I, like many golfers, had been drawn as much to the course as to the game itself.

I could remember the first golf course I ever played. It was a muni, not unlike Rock Creek Park. It was called Orchard Hills; it was in Paramus, New Jersey; and it is no longer there. The county government built a community college on the land years ago.

My father took me to Orchard Hills when he deemed me

old enough to start learning the game. He woke me up well before dawn on a summer day. He was determined that we should not hold up serious golfers and that we must, therefore, be on the course well before any of them were out of bed. We parked in an empty lot. He stuffed ten dollars for two greens fees into the pro shop mailbox and left a note explaining that we would sign in when we finished the front side.

I don't remember any of the shots I struck that day, though I do recall that my score for nine holes was 78. But I can remember the vista off the first tee. It was a par four with a broad fairway rising to a plateau green. The second hole was a par three heading down from that promontory, with a commanding view of a pond and the green beyond. In my mind's eye the grass at Orchard Hills is velvety and thick, though experience tells me that a municipal course in New Jersey probably had weedy turf chopped up with divot holes.

Velvety or not, I fell instantly in love with that landscape. I liked walking on it. I liked just looking at it. And I have felt the same way about almost every golf course I have seen since then. Something about the sight of a fairway both soothes and excites me.

I don't think this instinctive appreciation of lush, clipped grass is confined to golfers. Visit Versailles, the seventeenth-century palace of Louis XIII outside Paris, and you will see a *tapis vert* leading from the palace walls to the Fountain of Apollo. It looks like a great site for a short par four, maybe a three-wood and a wedge. I think that the designers of French palace gardens were pleasing some of the same instinctive tastes that a golf course pleases. They were appealing to the same instinct Dr. Lichtenberg had cited when he talked about the innate aesthetic appeal of the golf course.

One of the pitfalls of evolutionary biology, Bob Wright had written, is the temptation to compose "Just So" stories about the ancestral environment to explain modern phenomena. Such stories are precious and appealing, and they have the virtue of being hard to discredit. No *Australopithecus* is going to write a letter to the *Journal of Social and Biological Structures* saying, "No, I was there. You got it wrong."

Still, I was tempted to speculate about this apparently instinctive attraction of the golf course environment.

At some point in prehistory, it is clear, early man stopped being exclusively a forest dweller, like the chimps and gorillas. He ventured into other environments. Looking at Africa today, it is possible to envision what one of these environments must have been. At the edge of some forest, early man would have encountered savanna—brushy grasslands. Some portion of this grassland must have been clipped, kept short by grazing animals.

To some of these prehumans, this must have seemed a frightening environment in comparison to the comfort of the forest, where trees provided immediate refuge from a host of predators and where food—well, food grew on trees. They were like the chimps who wanted nothing to do with Jane Goodall or her camp, the chimps whose caution was stronger than their curiosity. They stayed in the forest.

But some portion of the hominid population had a gene or genes that made these grasslands seem more attractive. Perhaps they were simply curious. Perhaps they were actually drawn to the environment of short grass. This group would have ventured out of the forest and into the grasslands.

Once there, they would have gained significant advantages over their forest-bound brethren. Grass that has been clipped by grazing animals suggests the presence of a new source of food—gazelles and other hoofed animals—for those able to hunt it down. This meant that in periods when natural cycles made food scarce in the forest, a portion of humankind had a backup source of nourishment. This would have been a major advantage in the competition to survive. Moreover, the ability to provide food could have been a significant advantage for a male in the competition to procreate. Women have often been shown, when assessing potential mates and fathers, to favor men who can provide well for their offspring.

Thus, I thought, some substantial portion of humanity could have an instinctive attraction to the environment of the golf course.

I tried this theory on Bob as we trudged up the eighth hole, a par four to an elevated green. Bob had hit his customary high fade off the tee toward a copse of trees. He was looking not only for his ball but for "the shot that makes me come back," the well-struck ball that convinces the golfer that a good game is hidden within himself and all he has to do is find it more consistently.

Some people would have told me, with justification, to shut up and play golf. Bob is too kind for that. "There might be something to it," he said of my theory. Evolutionary psychologists, he went on, have been doing some speculating about the kinds of environments we are genetically wired to like.

Bob hit another push fade and asked me if I could see what he was doing wrong. This was a bit like asking Elizabeth Taylor for advice on building an enduring marriage. But I obliged by telling him that his grip looked a little weak—one can always sound sage on a golf course by analyzing someone else's grip.

Bob turned his left hand over a bit and hit a shot that flew straight. "Ah, the magic grip," he said, smiling. We walked on, climbing toward the elevated green.

Certain kinds of environments, Bob said, seem to repel most human beings. Most of us, for instance, instinctively want to stay away from swamps. There's a reason for this. Prehumans who had an instinctive attraction to swamps presumably suffered a disproportionate number of early deaths from the bites of insects, snakes, alligators, and other swamp denizens. They lost ground in the competition to pass their genes to the next generation. So succeeding generations had increasingly fewer genetic swamp lovers.

On the other hand, Bob said, there are certain environments that most people do favor. Many of us prefer what are called "prospect environments." These are high spots on open ground from which a hunter might see both prospective prey and prospective predators. An elevated tee on a golf course, for instance, is a good example of a prospect environment. I suspect that architects look for places to build elevated tees precisely because they have found that so many of their clients instinctively like them.

Some of us tend to prefer what are called refuge environments, wooded areas that offer opportunities to protect self and offspring by hiding or climbing trees. Obviously, this doesn't mean that some people necessarily like only woodlands or only grassy promontories. It's just a tendency.

We climbed onto the eighth green and I looked around. I could see neither bison nor tigers, but the vista was calming, soothing. In the distance the gang on the practice green cackled over some missed putt. "This would be a prospect environment," I said.

"Could be," Bob agreed.

We turned into a stretch of the course that offered lots of examples of both prospect and refuge environments, a series of holes cut through dense woods. There were oak trees as thick as boulders, entangled with vines. A couple of errant shots allowed me to inspect this environment more closely than I had wanted.

It occurred to me that the theory of prospect and refuge environments might explain one of the minor mysteries of a golfer's life—the way some nongolfers hate the game. I speak here not of people like Alex Beam, who don't know the game and prefer not to play but generally keep quiet about it unless asked. I speak of people who seem to seek out chances to criticize golf and people who play it, who find it difficult to pen a sentence containing the word "golf" that doesn't also contain the words "plaid pants."

Maureen Dowd of *The New York Times,* for instance, wrote

sullen little pieces from Kennebunkport about George Bush's golf outings when she covered the White House during his administration. Bush might have thought her dudgeon stemmed from her dislike of his politics. But she had no more use for Bush's successor, also a golfer. Her attitude seemed, in fact, to stem not so much from politics as from a difference in *Weltanschauung* between herself and the presidents she covered. Part of what defined that difference was golf. Dowd, I suspect, has no use for anyone who plays golf in much the same way that some wine connoisseurs have no use for anyone who likes beer, the way vegans have no use for lovers of barbecue, the way Alanis Morissette fans don't buy Aretha Franklin recordings. In a column published just before this particular round with Bob Wright in Rock Creek Park, she had defined golf as "men with guts pretending they were exercising."

In that column, though, she'd also made an interesting confession:

> *I committed my first sin on a golf course. When I was eight, my girlfriend and I devised a game where we would hide in the woods at Rock Creek Park Golf Course in Washington and wait for businessmen to hit over the hill. Then we'd run out, grab the balls and retreat to our bosky perch to watch the men search vainly for them.*

The hilly hole through the woods she had described coincidentally lay in front of me—No. 12, a tough par four. I was taking more strokes on the back nine, the result of the tight fairways and a reckless urge to play the driver. But I was thinking about this op-ed vitriol over golf. Freud, outdated though he might be, could perhaps have explained Dowd's urge to steal balls. What struck me was the juxtaposition of the two environments. The golfers strode on the grass. The golf hater crouched in the woods. It was not difficult to imagine a set of prehistoric ancestors, one group venturing out of the woods and another unwilling to do so, the latter seething in their refuge, perhaps later retreating to scratch dyspeptic glyphs into a flat rock.

"There's a book you ought to read," Bob told me as we toiled up the eighteenth hole. I was struggling to break eighty. "It's about the role of environment. There's a chapter in it by a man named Orians you might find helpful." A short time later he gave me a copy of the book, *The Biophilia Hypothesis.*

The Biophilia Hypothesis suggests that humankind has a deep-seated, presumably genetic need for contact with the natural world. This need goes beyond the simple physical demands for air and food. It's an esthetic requirement that manifests itself in countless ways we rarely bother to recognize—in the patches of lawn we struggle to maintain, in the millions of visits we pay each year to zoos, in the way the wealthy tend to build their houses on high ground with views of clear water and copses of trees.

Gordon Orians, an ornithologist from the University of Washington, was the co-author, with Judith Heerwagen, of one of the most pertinent of the book's essays, entitled "Humans, Habitats and Aesthetics." According to their thesis, most creatures face critical choices in the selection of habitat. If the creature chooses well, everything essential to life becomes easier—finding food, protecting itself from the elements and from predators, and ultimately, reproducing. The animals you see around you are genetically inclined to be pretty good at finding hospitable niches for themselves in the natural mosaic—because members of the species that weren't so inclined tended not to survive and have progeny. This process is instinctive. The migrating bird doesn't know why it chooses certain kinds of woodlands to nest in. It just does. Neither do humans consciously calculate what sort of surroundings they will find pleasant. They respond instinctively to certain objects, certain smells, certain sights.

Rarely did the humans in our ancestral environment find a single place that satisfied their needs permanently. More typically, they moved through a variety of micro-environments in search of food, water, and protection. They might inhabit a particular area when certain trees bore fruit or when game animals clustered there. When those trees were stripped or the animals migrated, the humans moved on. A year later they might return. They were cyclical wanderers.

Orians and Heerwagen theorized that modern men and women would tend to perceive environments differently because of the division of labor in this early, wandering human society—women being largely gatherers and men largely hunters. Females tended to favor protective, refuge environments like woodlands. Such places offered fruits and nuts for the finding. They offered protection for children, since the principal predators of early human beings—the large cats and hyenas—hunted mostly on open grasslands. Males tended to favor prospect environments, more open landscapes where game herds might graze. These were landscapes in which both predators and prey might be seen from a distance and in which scattered copses of trees provided potential refuge. This was the characteristic environment of the prehistoric savanna. The authors suggested that both sexes responded favorably to environments that offered the chance of easy movement-paths through the grass.

Since it is impossible to go back to the ancestral environment and test such hypotheses, Orians and Heerwagen looked for other methods to verify that these, in fact, are the landscape features people find instinctively attractive. They chose to study landscape art. In depictions of actual scenes, they looked particularly for ways in which the artist had changed an existing, real landscape to make the picture more appealing. In imaginary landscapes they tried to analyze the features each artist had felt impelled to create.

They studied 108 landscape paintings by Irish and French artists; 52 of the paintings were by female artists and 56 by males. Almost half of the women's landscapes had what they deemed to be a high incidence of places of refuge—houses or vegetative cover. Only 25 percent of the men's landscapes displayed this preference for places of refuge. The men were twice as likely as the women to paint landscapes with high places of prospect and broad views of the horizon.

They also studied the work of an eighteenth-century British landscape architect, Humphrey Repton. Repton's practice was to make before-and-after drawings for prospective clients showing their lands as they looked and as he thought they might like them to look after he finished redoing them. His drawings offer a glimpse at what a successful landscaper of that era found appealing to his clients.

More often than not, Repton's drawings proposed to change the existing landscape to give it many of the features of a golf course. He opened up dense woodlands and made them more savanna-like, drawing broad areas of grass interspersed with clusters of trees. But where his client already had unbroken, featureless pastureland, he added trees. Everywhere he opened up distant views, especially to the horizon. He added paths and bridges to suggest ease of movement. He added ponds. And he often broke up straight edges—an open field bordered by a straight line of woods. He made the straight edges uneven, placing trees the way a golf architect might create a dogleg hole.

Were the green vistas in Repton's work appealing to the same instinct that responds to fairways? Were the ponds he drew the equivalent of water hazards? And was the preference of male painters for places of prospect and of female painters for places of refuge caused by the same factor that causes the present population of golfers to be three-quarters male and one-quarter female?

It was impossible to tell, but I found the essay very suggestive. By e-mail I got in touch with Gordon Orians. As it happened, he was planning to attend a professional conference in Washington the following month and he would have a free evening. I invited him to my club for dinner.

Dr. Orians proved to be a genial dinner companion, a midwesterner without pretension. He was born in Wisconsin, the son of a Protestant minister. He recalled that his father had played a little golf, but he himself never had. When he was nine, his father had introduced him to birding and nature photography. He decided instantly to become an ornithologist. He remembered, as a nine-year-old, rising at 5:30 A.M. to go to the shore of Lake Michigan to watch birds for an hour, returning home for a bite of breakfast, and then going off to school.

Dr. Orians still had an apparently insatiable curiosity about birds and the natural world. He was the sort of person who would take his family to Costa Rica for a vacation. Sitting on the beach with his children, he would begin to observe the way brown pelicans catch fish. He would notice that year-old pelicans catch them less skillfully than older birds. He would return home and write a paper offering evidence that birds, like humans, can learn skills.

His specialty was red-winged blackbirds, which are common in the Northwest. His observations of the way they choose particular environments had led him to the study of the way human beings make similar choices and to the study I had read about in *The Biophilia Hypothesis.*

"It's not a frivolous notion that a golf course represents an attractive habitat," he said. "After all, people spend inordinate sums of money on 'dream vacations' that take them to environments like those of our tropical origins—lush with water, green trees, flowers, and grass."

Our dinner done, we stepped out of the dining room and walked across the terrace toward the first tee of the golf course. It was early evening. The sun had gone down, but it was not quite dark. The course was deserted, but its major features were still visible—the broad swaths of closely mown fairway, the dark clumps of evergreens, the thicker grass of the rough. The absence of players and some of the modern detritus that's been introduced to the game—the puttering golf carts and the titanium clubs and the cell phones—seemed to invite us to consider the course as an environment, independent of the game. Maybe that's among the reasons why some golfers find the carts and the phones so annoying. They interfere with that consideration.

"This is an African savanna," Dr. Orians exclaimed as we walked off the tee.

The low grass, he said, would be the most attractive feature of this environment for an early hominid because of its suggestion that grazing animals were nearby. He would have walked out on it with primitive digging tools and clubs, searching for food—edible roots, animals, even carcasses. Early man was a scavenger. Dr. Orians agreed that those hominids who found the savanna attractive, who ventured into it, would have gained a substantial advantage in the competition to survive and reproduce over those who preferred to stay in the forest.

We ended our outward walk well short of the landing area for good tee shots and still a couple of hundred yards from that place of prospect otherwise known as the first green. We headed back to the dining room for a last cup of coffee.

It was, we agreed, entertaining to speculate about the nature of a golf course. It could well be that when we step onto one, we are reenacting the steps taken by some hominid a hundred thousand generations in the past, steps that helped him or her become our ancestor. It could even be that the clubs we carry remind us, on some instinctive level, of the tools they carried in their search for food. But in the end this line of inquiry can produce only speculation. We can't know.

We can only know that there is something within some of us that tells us, when we first step onto a golf course, even a course as modest as Rock Creek Park or old Orchard Hills, that we are in a good and auspicious place.

What I Learned from Bob Rotella

Most of the difficulties of golf are mental, not physical.

—Haultain

Hitting a golf ball plucks a string somewhere within us, and hitting it well strums a chord. Walking onto a golf course puts us in touch with our roots, edible and otherwise. Both propositions are true, but they don't explain golf's capacity to become an obsession. Hitting the golf ball and walking the golf course are like moving bishops diagonally and rooks horizontally in chess. Moving the pieces in accordance with the rules may be chess, but it isn't playing chess. And the pleasure of the elemental physical acts of golf only begins to explain the game's appeal.

Anyone who has played golf for very long discovers a curious fact about the physical elements of the game. They're hard, but they're not that hard. By the time a golfer has played enough to break a hundred, he's already caught a tee shot just right and driven it, say, two hundred and sixty yards down the middle. He's drilled a seven-iron to tap-in range. He's holed a chip shot, and he's sunk a forty-foot putt. He's played shots, in other words, that would win the U.S. Open for him if he

could just string about two hundred and eighty of them together.

Compare this to other sports.

Only an insignificant sliver of the general population will
ever leap from the foul line, twist in the air, and stuff the ball
through the basket with a reverse tomahawk jam. An equally
small number could hold off a blitzing National Football
League linebacker, return a Pete Sampras serve, or run the
hundred meters in less than ten seconds. We are simply physically incapable of competing on the highest level of most
sports, in part because most sports match individuals against
one another. Only the strongest and the fastest survive. As far
as the rest of us are concerned, in most sports the spirit may
be willing but the flesh is weak.

In golf it's the other way around. We know that our bodies
are capable of producing the requisite shots. We just can't get
our brains to make our bodies produce them, at least not often enough, not consistently enough. This criticality of the
brain is what makes golf the most enticing of sports. Great
golf seems always within the reach of the body and only
rarely within the grasp of the mind. To play golf well, a golfer
need only master himself, need only discipline his own brain.
I use the word *only* advisedly. Because, of course, mastering
oneself and disciplining one's own mind are the greatest of
challenges, for all their seeming simplicity. When we do manage to make the brain the servant of our golf games, the satisfaction is profound. We play in search of that satisfaction.

I had sensed all this in a vague way. But my education in
the mental side of golf did not begin until I met Dr. Bob
Rotella. From him I learned that to say, as Haultain did, that
most of the difficulties of golf are mental is only to scratch
the surface of the psychology of the game.

I met Rotella by a fortuitous accident. He was planning to
write a book on how winning golfers think, with the assis-
tance of Bob Carney of *Golf Digest*. But just as the project
was about to start, Carney got a promotion, and his new job

did not allow him the time he would need to work with Rotella. Carney asked out of the deal. Rotella therefore asked Rafe Sagalyn, his literary agent, if he could recommend another writer. Rafe happened to have a writer on his client list who liked to play golf—me. "This guy knows how to help golfers win," Rafe told me. "Go on down to Charlottesville and meet him. See if you could work together."

If anything, I knew less then about psychology than I knew about golf. My concept of a psychologist's work had been formed by a couple of brief encounters with therapists, a cursory reading of the more accessible works of Freud, and a lot of bad movies. I thought that a sports psychologist, like the analysts of the cinema, would likely have a goatee, a tweed jacket, and a pipe. He would invite his golfing clients to lie down on a couch in an office lined with framed diplomas, books, and abstract or carefully neutral paintings. He would encourage them to talk about their childhood. I imagined that at some point in a successful course of therapy, the patient would gain an insight along the lines of "That's it! I miss my short putts because I resent the way my parents toilet-trained me!" The patient would rise from the couch reborn and enlightened, return to the Tour, and choke no more.

I could not have been more mistaken. Rotella lived with his wife, Darlene, and their daughter, Casey, in a comfortable ranch house a couple of miles from the grounds of the University of Virginia, where he taught. It was the sort of home in which the living room and the dining room were rarely used. Family life centered around the kitchen and a couple of casually furnished adjacent rooms, adorned with golf magazines and trophies. A set of hand dumbbells rested on the hearth. Rotella himself looked nothing like the stereotypical therapist. He was compact, wiry, and athletic, with a calm smile and black hair. He wore sweaters and slacks. The only hint of the academic about him was his eyeglasses.

"Some guys call me Bob and some call me Doc," he said. "Use whatever makes you comfortable."

He invited me downstairs to the basement. The room we entered had no desk, no diplomas. There was a universal gym. There was a putting cup sunk into the floor, surrounded by a mixed array of putters and golf balls. And the pictures on the walls were hardly neutral, hardly abstract. Above the chair where Rotella often sat hung a copy of the famed Hy Peskin photo of Ben Hogan following through on a one-iron shot to the seventy-second green of the U.S. Open he won at Merion in 1950. Framed, autographed magazine cover pictures of Rotella clients hoisting trophies lined the stairwell. Rotella had helped some of the best players in the game, from Tom Kite to Davis Love III, win major championships. He didn't need to hang his diplomas on the wall. Their testimonials said all that needed to be said about his credentials.

Rotella's career path, I learned, was as distinctive as his office. He grew up in Rutland, Vermont. His paternal grandparents were immigrants from Sicily. His grandfather died young, crushed beneath a falling block of marble at a stoneworks in Rutland. Rotella's father, Guido, had to go to work at an early age, and there was not enough money for him to finish his education. He became a barber. He and his wife, Laura, had five children, although if they were editing this text, they would ask me to write "were blessed with five children." That's the sort of people they are.

For as long as he could remember, sport had fascinated Bob Rotella, and he was quite successful as an athlete. He played quarterback for his high school football team. He was a guard on the basketball team. At Castleton State College in Vermont, he continued with basketball and was twice elected captain. He was a small-college All-American in lacrosse.

Rotella, though, did not see himself as physically gifted. When I had occasion to ask him to talk about his own athletic career, he was likely to offer a story like the one about the junior varsity basketball coach at his high school who cut him from the squad and told him he didn't have enough size or talent to play. Rotella saw himself as a person of average physical ability who had made himself successful in sport by dint of practice and careful attention to the proper way to play a game. He was the classic athletic overachiever, the kind of kid who seems too short and too slow but who makes himself valuable by hustling all the time, by learning to hit the open man, to lay down the sacrifice bunt. He saw his athletic career as a lesson in the virtues of persistence and dedication.

From an early age, he told me, he had loved to listen to the coaches who imparted those virtues. He picked their brains to find out how they instilled motivation and confidence. He understood very early in the process that the genius of successful coaches rarely lies in the plays they devise. It lies in the way they motivate their players to execute those plays. That was the side of coaching that fascinated Rotella. His ideal was Vince Lombardi.

When he finished college, he wanted to become a coach. He got a job handling the junior varsity team at his old high school, the same team from which he'd been cut as a freshman. And he was a very good coach. He might, I suspect, still be producing confident, motivated, state championship basketball teams in Vermont if he hadn't taken a second job teaching swimming and athletic skills to children with mental disabilities at the Brandon Training School.

Rotella responded strongly to those kids' enthusiasm and desire to learn. He found immense satisfaction in helping a child who was committed to improvement but didn't quite know how to go about it. He taught such children patiently and thoroughly. Because neither he nor they accepted the diagnosis that they could not learn, they did learn. His success attracted the attention of some educators from the University of Connecticut, and they invited him to enter their graduate school.

The field of sports psychology was just emerging in those years, and Rotella was one of its pioneers. Instinctively, he turned away from the kind of analysis that permeated mainstream psychology and psychiatry at the time. He read and largely rejected the then-fashionable doctrines of Freud and B. F. Skinner. He became neither a Freudian nor a Skinnerite. Instead, he retained his belief in the coaches' principles he'd learned as an athlete. When he finished his doctoral work, he was a Lombardian with a Ph.D.

The University of Virginia hired him to teach sports psychology in its school of education. Informally, he began working with the athletic program. Up until that time, in the mid-1970s, Virginia, athletically, was a school with excellent architecture and storied fraternity parties. Its football and basketball teams had some talent, but they generally found ways to lose. They fumbled on the opponent's goal line. They missed their foul shots in the final seconds.

After Rotella arrived, that began to change. The basketball team won a conference championship and went twice to the NCAA Final Four. The football team started going to bowl games. Rotella, obviously, was not the only factor in this improvement. But he was a major factor, teaching the Virginia athletes how to get the most out of themselves under pressure.

It was not until he had established himself in sports like basketball and football that Rotella turned to golf. He had caddied as a boy, but golf clubs and lessons were beyond his family's means. He was an adult neophyte in the game.

He applied himself to it with the rigor and persistence he had learned in other sports. Rotella would not permit me to write much about his own golf skills in the books we collaborated on. The code he grew up with prohibited bragging. But he had made himself a superb golfer, a scratch player who had won several regional amateur titles in Virginia. He was not overly long off the tee, but he was consistent. And having analyzed the game and determined that putting, chipping, and pitching were the most vital elements in a player's score, he made himself excellent on and around the green. He was his own best advertisement for the techniques and ideas he taught.

This athletic background and ability to play golf helped Rotella immensely when he started consulting with professional golfers. The forebears of the present generation of tournament golfers, men like Snead and Hogan, Palmer and Nicklaus, knew little or nothing about psychology in the academic sense of the word, though they had all, through trial and error, learned to think effectively. If they had ever consulted a psychologist, they would surely have kept that fact to themselves. The current generation, having come of age in the 1970s and 1980s, was a bit more open-minded on the subject of counseling. But Rotella, as he began his work with professional golfers, had to persuade them that he was not just some egghead with a bunch of theories. His golf game helped do that for him. Unlike nearly everyone else in the world who holds a Ph.D. in psychology, Rotella could take a professional golfer out on the golf course and play with him—not necessarily on an even basis, but close enough. After a professional saw Rotella get up and down a half-dozen times in the course of a round, shoot a score around 70, and perhaps win a little of his money, the professional was usually quite ready to listen to Rotella's theories about how a successful golfer thinks.

During my work on our first book together, *Golf Is Not a Game of Perfect,* I flew to Akron to interview one of Rotella's longtime clients and close friends, Brad Faxon, at the World Series of Golf. Faxon took me out on the practice tee, and we happened to be standing next to Curtis Strange, the two-time U.S. Open champion. Faxon introduced us and told Strange why I was there.

Strange was hitting drivers off the tee, shot after shot with a precise little fade at the end. "Rotella, huh?" he said between shots. He set up, swung, and we watched the ball fly toward the end of the range.

"I don't believe in that psychology crap," Strange continued, turning as he spoke to take another golf ball from his caddie. He teed the ball up and addressed it. Then he looked at me. "Rotella, though—he's been in the arena. I'll listen to a guy like him."

By the time I met him, Rotella had established a practice that would soon cause him to quit teaching at the University and devote full time to helping people—not just golfers, but businesspeople, entertainers, and others who had heard that Rotella knew how to help them get the most from their abilities. When he accepted a new client, he generally invited him or her to come to Charlottesville for a couple of days of intensive work. The client moved into the guest suite in the Rotella basement and became, in effect, a temporary member of the family.

If the client was a golfer, Rotella would spend some time talking to him about his aspirations and his problems. He might work on the player's putting, using the cup in the basement floor. Generally, he'd take him to a golf course nearby, play a few holes, and start imparting the habits of thought that characterize winning golfers.

Many of his clients were well-known pros. But a number were unknown amateurs. I found that Rotella didn't care much whether a client had the game to win the U.S. Open or was striving only for a club championship. What mattered to Rotella was that the client was striving. He seemed to have only limited interest in people who wanted a couple of quick tips to cure their putting yips. But he would spend hours working with someone who was committed to becoming the best player she could be, had put in the practice time, but had run up against a mental obstacle.

Patsy Price was such a golfer. After the publication of *Golf Is Not a Game of Perfect*, we heard via the Internet from readers who had found the book helpful to their game. When we started working on the sequel, *Golf Is a Game of Confidence*, I invited two readers, Fred Arenstein and Patsy, to come to Charlottesville, play a round of golf with Rotella, and recount their experiences. Those conversations subsequently helped us write chapters in the new book.

Patsy was a short, strong, and athletic woman who'd become passionate about golf after her thirtieth birthday. Her dream was to have a single-digit handicap and to qualify for the Women's Amateur in California, where she lived. She took lessons, and she insisted that the pros who taught her explain why they were asking her to swing the club a certain way as well as how to swing it. She practiced. She and her husband, Dave, had a net in their living room for winter drills.

During the round she played with Rotella, it became evident that Patsy could smack the ball. She hit her tee shots more than two hundred yards, generally straight down the fairway. But she had some kind of phobia about her irons. As often as not, she shanked them, hit them fat, or in some other way wasted the chance her tee shot had given her to make a par.

It was a chilly November day, and when the round and the conversation were over, Rotella could have shaken Patsy's hand, thanked her for coming, and headed home for a cup of hot tea. She wasn't, after all, a client. But he invited her to the practice range and got a bucket of balls. And he worked with her for an hour until she stopped shanking the ball and started hitting her irons as well as she hit her woods. That was the sort of thing he enjoyed.

Rotella, I realized, saw himself as a kind of Sherpa. He helped people reach heights they could not have attained on their own. He pointed out paths, offered encouragement. Occasionally he got behind someone and pushed.

Rotella was secure enough in his ideas that he didn't modify them when a player he worked with seemed to be floundering. I flew out to Phoenix one January weekend to work with him on a manuscript. He was there consulting with players at the Phoenix Open. He told me to meet him at a California Pizza Kitchen across the road from his hotel. When I got there, he was finishing dinner with a player with whom he'd been working since the player was a collegian.

This player had suffered what seemed to me to be a series of mental lapses. To put it less euphemistically, he seemed to have a choking problem. He'd finished second seven times on the Tour. But his seconds were, in several cases, inglorious seconds. He'd held a lead and blown it during the final holes. He was, I would have thought, a player who needed to try something new in his thinking.

Rotella thought differently. After the player had left, I asked him what he'd told him.

"I told him he was doing all the right things. He just has to keep doing them and be patient," Rotella said.

The player was David Duval. Six months later he won his first tournament and began a run of success that took him to the top of the world rankings.

Rotella was a competent writer who had already published several books. But his schedule didn't give him much time for writing. He wanted a collaborator, and we agreed to work together. My job initially was to review the notes, audiotapes, and videotapes he had made from some of the sessions he'd conducted with golfers. Then I would interview him to ask the clarifying questions I thought an average golfer would pose. Then I sorted the material into logical sequence and wrote a draft. Largely the draft amounted to edited transcripts of what Rotella had said to me and to others.

Much of what I read and heard in this process was a revelation to me, even though I had been playing golf, off and on, for nearly thirty years. Rotella started from Haultain's conclusion that both the challenge and the fascination of golf were largely mental. But he explored that territory and mined it in ways Haultain had never imagined. That part of golf played between the ears, as outlined by Rotella, was like a Russian *matryoshka,* or nesting doll—an affair of many layers.

First and most obvious were the calculations required to plan a shot. What club to use? How far to hit the ball? How would wind and weather affect its flight? On good courses, which present the player with many options, these calculations were always complex. But they were still the simplest of the problems that engaged the player's mind.

Far knottier were the mental problems of the next layer, the problems related to executing that shot, to making the body produce its best swing. The question of the player's nerves under pressure—of choking—intensified and complicated this aspect of the game to roughly the same degree that the absence of oxygen complicates space travel.

The harder we try to force our brains to master the problem of golf, the more difficult the problem becomes. One way to make golfers try harder is to ratchet up the stakes. Give me two-foot putts on the practice green, and I will make a dozen in a row. Put me in the last group of my club's B-team match (the result of which will garner all of a single line of agate type in the next morning's newspaper), make the two-footer worth half a point for the team, and I will quite possibly yank it past the hole. Put Greg Norman in the final round of the Masters with a six-stroke lead, and the same body that produced a 63 on Thursday produces a 78. So there's at least one thing my game has in common with Greg Norman's. We have both been taught through bitter experience that the quality of one's golf can fluctuate in inverse proportion to the desire to play well.

Rotella had simple, sensible approaches to these problems. For instance, he suggested that serious players prepare a game plan for a competitive round, making judgments ahead of time about the way to attack the course. That requires some time and preparation, but it helps with the first of the mental challenges, the strategy and tactics of play. A good player usually doesn't get to the tee on the last hole of the U.S. Open and decide then and there whether to hit driver. He thinks about the options beforehand and devises a plan with alternatives for every conceivable variable—where he stands in the tournament, the wind and weather, how well he's been hit-

ting the ball. That way, he makes critical decisions coolly. He
has the sense that he's merely executing a plan as he goes
about his round.

Rotella's answer to the second problem, the problem that
comes down to nerves, grew from his knowledge of the way
the body and mind work together. The body seems to work
best without a lot of conscious thought. If you drive a car
with a manual transmission, you already know this. If you
think hard and carefully about the sequence of sensory cues,
eye, hand, and foot movements required to shift gears, you'll
likely revert to driving the way you did when you were
learning and had no choice but to think about those things.
The car will lurch down the street or stall completely. But if
you assume you already have mastered the skill and just do it,
you'll shift smoothly.

Or consider the balance beam. If you put a balance beam
on the floor, any reasonably coordinated person can get on it
at one end and walk to the other. Put the beam fifteen feet in
the air, though, and walking its length becomes much more
challenging. The reason is that people are afraid of falling. In
their fear they get cautious, careful, and analytical about the
way they perform the simple task of putting one foot in front
of the other. By doing so, they rob themselves of their natural
grace and balance.

Hitting a golf ball is more complicated than shifting gears
or walking a balance beam, of course. But Rotella believed
that when a golfer succumbed to nerves, it was really a matter of thinking about the wrong things, just as the person on
the elevated balance beam did. As Rotella liked to put it, such
a golfer "turned on the conscious mind." He got careful, cautious, and analytical about his swing. And like the person on
the elevated beam, he robbed himself of his natural grace. The
extraneous thoughts that led to this condition might be
about the money he stood to win or lose. They might be
about the humiliation of defeat. They might be about the
mechanics of drawing the club back and striking the ball.

At any time in a round of golf, but especially under pressure, Rotella believed it was a mistake to think of the mechanics of the swing, just as it would be a mistake to shift your attention from the road to the depth to which your left foot depresses the clutch pedal. It was better to focus on a very small target, think about the ball going there, and then swing, trusting that your skill would be sufficient to execute the shot.

There were no guarantees that this would work. But a golfer who thought this way at least preserved the possibility of bringing his full complement of grace and rhythm to the shot at hand. He had a better chance of pulling off a shot than a golfer who stood over the ball and tried to recall what Hogan had said about the position of the wrists at the top of the backswing. The time to think about the wrists, Rotella preached, was during practice—not on the course. He was a firm believer in lessons and practice. But tinkering with the swing belonged on the practice range.

This was a revelation to me. I was the sort of golfer who knew very little about the mechanics of the swing except for the few shibboleths that everyone hears—keep the head down, keep the left arm straight. My ignorance, of course, didn't stop me from trying to diagnose my swing problems and fix them in the middle of every round I played. I was constantly discovering new cures for my slice—a different stance, a different grip. They worked for a shot or two, if they worked at all. And then things usually got worse as I tightened up and lost whatever rhythm I'd brought to the course. I was the sort of player who needed Rotella's advice.

Rotella's other ideas about grace under pressure were equally sensible. He believed that following a precise routine before every shot helped achieve consistency and helped block out extraneous thoughts. He believed in being conservative in strategy and bold and decisive in the execution of every shot. He spoke of the futility of anger and the advisability of immediately forgetting bad shots and concentrating on the shot at hand.

But he did not believe one of the principal ideas that Haultain had put forward in 1908. Haultain wrote, "In golf, there is never any reflex action possible. Every stroke must be played by the mind."

Rotella, coming to golf from a background in other sports, disagreed. He felt that good golfers had a lot in common with all good athletes, including reflex action. They looked at their target and, without delay, they swung the club. They didn't think about how to swing and then swing. They just did it, much the way a batter reacts to a pitched ball or a quarterback focuses on a receiver's numbers and drills the ball there. When he was advising Davis Love III on how to improve his short game, Rotella asked Love to think about his friend Michael Jordan playing basketball. Jordan didn't look at the basket and think about what to do. He looked and shot in one seamless effort. Love needed to do the same thing on his chip shots: look at the hole and react.

Rotella knew that most golfers were addicted to swing thoughts, that they felt they had to have something in mind as they swung. He told his clients they could have one swing thought if they must, but only one. And it ought to be something simple, like "Take it back slow," instead of something more complex and mechanical, like "Rotate the forearms on the downswing." Ideally, he counseled, they would reach a state of mental discipline where they needed no swing thoughts as they played.

This made sense to me because it reminded me of my mental state during the infrequent hot streaks I found myself in on the golf course. There were occasions when I strung together three or four pars in a row. As I thought back to them, I recalled that during those streaks, I didn't think at all about how to swing the club. I just saw where I wanted to hit the ball and swung, confident that I could get it there. There was

a delicious sense of being in control. My little streaks generally ended as soon as a shot confounded my confident expec-
tations. Then I went back to trying to fix my swing and
hacking up the golf course. Rotella was saying that a golfer
could choose to think all the time the way he thought when
he happened to be on a hot streak. If he did, he improved the
chances of getting hot again.

As I studied Rotella's tapes and notes, it struck me that in
another sense Haultain had been right about the centrality of
mental struggle in the game. There were dozens of things a
golfer could think about as he walked to his ball and prepared
to hit a shot. Some were essential—target, yardage, wind,
club, and line of flight. For some shots he had to plot a trajectory. On the green he had to take into account the slope and
the speed. He had to decide when it was wise to aim at a pin
and go for a birdie and when it was wise to play safe. But
there were other thoughts Rotella categorized as harmful
distractions.

Part of the fascination of the game was that its leisurely nature gave you time to think of all those things. The frantic
pace of a football play or a fast break in basketball or the
speed of a pitched ball in baseball all but eliminated the possibility of conscious thought. Golf was just the opposite. The
player controlled the pace of the game. He could think as
much as he wanted about whatever he wanted before he
struck the ball.

More than that, golf tempted you to think of all the wrong
things. How frequently had I stood on an eighteenth tee
thinking that I needed only a bogey to make a certain score
instead of thinking about where I wanted to hit the ball?
How often had I stood over a putt thinking about how I'd
pushed the last one past the hole? How often had I taken the
club back thinking, "Don't hit it in the water," then laid sod
over the ball and done just that?

What Rotella offered was a method for disciplining the
mind so that it focused on the right things. It was not, he

pointed out, a perfect method. The mind, after all, was an imperfect organism. Even the best players, in the midst of their best rounds, lost their mental discipline at times and had to struggle to regain it. Brad Faxon told me about the 63 he'd shot in the final round of the 1995 PGA, a score that earned him a spot on the American Ryder Cup team. Even then, he recalled, he'd lost focus a couple of times, thinking about making the team or shooting 59, instead of strictly focusing on the shot at hand. His 63 might have been a 62 or 61.

To Rotella that was one of the glories of the game. In this respect he agreed with Haultain. Every round challenged the golfer to discipline his mind. No faster, stronger opponent was going to prevent him from doing so, the way a faster, stronger opponent might thwart him in football or basketball. The game's essential struggle was played out between the golfer's ears, where he had, or should have had, complete dominion.

That dominion was chimerical as often as not. Nearly every mind had a breaking point, a point at which it refused to behave properly. For someone like me it might come after a couple of presses in a two-dollar Nassau. For professionals it might come during the final round of Ryder Cup matches. But there was always a breaking point.

As I studied Rotella's ideas and started to incorporate them into my own game, my scores started to improve. I'd been playing in the low nineties. I started to play in the mid-eighties. It was a modest improvement, a leap from below average to average, but I was proud of it. And when, one day after several hours in the basement tape-recording my questions and his answers, he suggested that we play a round of golf together, I was eager to show him how well I was doing.

That eagerness, of course, was enough to push my undisciplined mind well past its breaking point. We went over to Rotella's club and started to play. Or rather, he did. My mind had turned to mush and my body had become spastic. Within a few holes it was as if every time I pulled a club from my bag

I was thinking, "What is this strange tool and how am I sup-posed to use it?"

Mercifully, I remember only a couple of the many terrible shots I hit that day. The most typical came on a short par four, a birdie hole for Rotella. A broad drainage ditch ran in front of the tee. Taking an iron because I had been hitting my woods so badly, I tried simply to get the ball somewhere into the fairway. Instead, I foozled it into the ditch. But the ball was in sight and the ditch was dry. Rotella stopped the cart on the bridge while, cheeks burning, I scrambled down with my wedge to try to hit a recovery shot. The ball lay in thick rough, and I took a mighty swing. It came out hot, low and left. With a thonk it hit one of the wooden posts supporting the cart bridge. It caromed back-ward, still hot, and flew within six inches of Rotella's chin. Then it disappeared into a thicket of bushes and trees.

Instead of showing him how my game had improved, I'd come within inches of braining him. If I'd had a caddie, he would've needed to know the Heimlich maneuver, I was choking so badly.

Rotella didn't flinch.

"Why don't you drop one in the fairway?" he asked kindly.

Rotella, I guess, was familiar with the kind of golf I was playing. He does much of his work on the Tour on Tuesdays and Wednesdays, the days before the tournaments start. Those are the days when the touring pros play with amateurs in charity events. The first tee at a pro-am is not usually a pretty place. Men and women who are reasonably competent golfers, people of means who can afford to pay several thou-sand dollars to play in a pro-am event, turn into bumbling hackers when they have to put their games on display before a handful of spectators and a professional. They think about the wrong things. They pass their breaking points.

Suddenly I sympathized with them.

Rotella had no magic pill to cure choking. The profession-als he worked with did not always close the deal when they had the lead in a tournament on Sunday, though they almost always began performing better under pressure after they worked with him than they had before. He couldn't make nerves disappear. The best he could do was help a player to welcome them, to understand that nervousness is a sign of engagement, evidence that the game we're playing is important. I found that helpful. I still felt nervous when I played in competition at the club, but I started to like being nervous.

Both chastened and impressed, I got to work on the first draft of the book that became *Golf Is Not a Game of Perfect*. As I delved further into Rotella's material and supplemented it by reading the autobiographies of some of the great players, I realized that many of them had arrived at similar conclusions. Stewart Maiden, a Scottish immigrant, taught young Bob Jones not to think about swing mechanics back at the turn of the century. Byron Nelson had come upon much the same idea by trial and error when he learned the game in the 1930s. Rotella had built on their ideas, adding the experience he'd had teaching athletes in other sports and the research data that was accumulating as the field of sports psychology grew and matured. What he taught, what I was writing, was based on the oldest and best traditions in the game.

The first draft talked about training your swing on the practice tee, then trusting it on the course. It spoke of selecting small targets. It spoke of game plans. I cataloged all the techniques Rotella taught for disciplining the mind during a round of golf. The draft built a case indirectly for the argument that golf fascinates us because it is, of all our games, the most demanding and stimulating of our brains.

I mailed it off to him. A week later I went down to Charlottesville to review it with him.

"It's fine," Rotella said, being tactful. "But it's not what I'm about. We have to revise it."

Dreams, Rotella explained. Where was the material about dreams? And free will. I had ignored the role of free will.

Another layer of the mental game unfolded. I had, indeed, heard Rotella say on the tapes that he wanted to know about a golfer's dreams, his ambitions, his goals. Dreams fueled commitment, and commitment was essential for a golfer's progress. And I had heard him speak of the centrality of a golfer's free will. Rotella believed firmly in the idea of free will, which was part of his religious upbringing. He believed that people could choose how they thought. Golfers, it followed, could choose to think in ways that helped them, could reject thoughts that distracted them.

I had heard those things, but I had considered them rhetorical flourishes, not as substantive or as useful as Rotella's advice on the various strategies for playing the short par five.

They were not, in Rotella's mind, flourishes. They were the elements of golf that justified the sweat and tears and the hours people invested in the game. They were a still deeper layer of the *matryoshka*. Trying to help me understand, Rotella told me more about Tom Kite.

Kite was one of the first prominent golfers to consult Rotella. Their association had begun more than a decade before. They were similar men, about the same age. Kite was five feet, eight inches tall and weighed one hundred and fifty-five pounds, about Rotella's size. He wore eyeglasses, like Rotella.

As golfers, they were also similar. Kite was never one of the longest hitters on the PGA Tour. But he was one of the best wedge players, the sort of golfer who couldn't reach some of the par fives in two shots but made birdies anyway by sticking his pitch close and holing the ensuing putt.

More important, he was Rotella's kind of athlete, a person of less-than-overwhelming physical gifts who made himself into a great golfer by respecting his dreams and applying his will. Kite was famous for the time he spent practicing. Rotella told me of all-day sessions he'd witnessed at Kite's home course in Austin, under a burning sun. Kite had sweated for every dollar he'd earned, and he was, at the time, the leader on the Tour's career earnings list.

Kite's dreams had included a major championship. He

came close to winning one in 1989, in the U.S. Open at Oak Hill in Rochester, leading by a stroke after rounds of 67, 69, and 69. But on the fifth hole in the final round, disaster struck. Kite blocked a ball right, into a rain-swollen creek. He'd taken seven on the hole and blown his chance to win.

What impressed Rotella was what Kite did after that. He vowed that he would never block a ball under pressure again. He found a teacher and changed his swing, widening his stance and flattening his swing plane. For an established professional, a man who'd already led the Tour in earnings, it was a radical and risky move.

For the better part of two years, Kite labored to master his new swing. Finally, in the wind at Pebble Beach in the 1992 U.S. Open, it paid off. He won his cherished major championship. For the better part of the next year, till he hurt his back in 1993, he was the best player in the world.

Rotella loved not so much the achievement itself but the strength of character it had required. Since his boyhood, people had told Kite he didn't have the talent to achieve his dreams in golf. (One of his boyhood rivals was Ben Crenshaw, and Crenshaw had always seemed to be the more talented of the two. How many people are likely to see future greatness in the second-best junior at their club?) Kite had stubbornly refused to listen to them. He simply kept grinding away. Ultimately, he succeeded. He embodied two virtues Rotella greatly admired, patience and perseverance.

It would not have mattered if Kite had applied himself to another sport, Rotella said. He could have been an All-American basketball player if that had been his dream.

"Wait a minute," I said. "Kite's short. He's nearsighted. I don't see any reason to think he can jump very high or run particularly fast. What makes you think he could have been an All-American basketball player?"

"If that's what he'd wanted to do, he'd have found a way," Rotella insisted.

I went home and wrote a second, revised draft. As I did, I

reflected on what Rotella had taught me and what it said about why people played golf.

What he meant, I realized, was that Kite had the sort of character that needed to strive. If Kite had not had golf, his character would have expressed itself in something else. Maybe, as Rotella contended, he could have become a champion in another sport. Maybe he would have become one of the trial lawyers dividing up the Texas tobacco settlement.

But Kite gravitated to golf, and that was not, I think, a coincidence. Golf is a great sport for the striver.

First, it has objective measures and standards by which the player can assess himself. Each hole produces a number. And while luck and chance affect the score a player achieves on a particular hole, luck and chance start to even out over eighteen holes. A seventy-two hole event of the sort the pros play generally identifies the man playing best in that particular week. Stroke averages and money earnings over the course of a season and a career give a professional a still more accurate, sometimes harshly accurate, picture of his own performance.

On the amateur level golf gives the striver similar criteria with which to measure himself. He has the number he posts after every round. If he plays regularly, he probably has a handicap based on the ten best scores he has posted in his last twenty rounds. Most of the regular players I know are strivers, and they pay close attention to these numbers. On the first tee they can tell you, to the nearest tenth of a stroke, their current handicap. They can tell you what their handicap was at the beginning of the season and what they'd like it to be at the end. They can tell you at the turn of each round where they stand in relation to par. They can tell you, on the eighteenth green, the score they'll make for the round if they sink their first putt. They may play four-ball matches, but they carefully keep their individual scores.

(Rotella, in fact, would classify this focus on numbers as a distraction. He'd point out that the best players, on their best days, often don't know what they've shot till they add the strokes up. On the course they focus only on each shot.)

Other sports offer statistical measurements. But in most cases, they're affected by what others do. A quarterback's completion percentage depends on the skill of his receivers, the plays the coach calls, and the performance of the opposing defense. A basketball player's scoring average may or may not reflect the contribution he makes to his team. And it may change for the worse if the team decides to run plays that set someone else up with shots. Good pitching beats good hitting. Winning 6-2, 6-2 in tennis means nothing by itself; its worth depends on how well the opposition played.

In some sports the score depends on judging. How is a gymnast or a diver to know if his score from one performance to the next reflects a real change in his performance or just the tastes of a particular set of judges?

The golfer knows. That knowledge spurs the striver on.

The striver finds that golf lends itself very well to the pursuit of improvement. He need not find someone to hit balls to him, as a tennis player must. He needs only his clubs, a practice area, and the urge to get better. He can put in hours of practice if he can allocate the time and summon the will to do it. That was what Kite had done.

For Rotella this was one of the best things about golf. It couldn't be said that golf requires sterling character. Too many reprobates have played the game well. But golf does tend to reward virtues like diligence and persistence. It may even help golfers develop them.

There is no guarantee, of course, that putting in hours of practice will win the U.S. Open. If there were, driving ranges would be open twenty-four hours a day. The correlation between effort and improvement is imperfect. But a correlation does exist. I'd seen that in my own game.

Rotella understood that people need to strive. They are happiest when they are working toward a goal. In our distant ancestors this trait helped assure survival. In our time survival is rarely an issue. Most of us needn't strive much to take care of rudimentary food and shelter. Yet the striving trait lives on within us, seeking an outlet. This is why people try to circumnavigate the globe in a hot-air balloon. It is why we have tourists trekking to the top of Mount Everest. It is why each autumn the marathons in New York and Washington are oversubscribed. People want to strive. Striving makes them happy. Therefore golf makes them happy.

This explains in part why so many people take up golf, or resume playing, in their thirties and forties. In their twenties people find ample opportunities to strive in other areas of life. On the job they may be pushing to get past the entry level. Promotions are available. There's tenure to get, or partnership. There are first houses to buy, cars to acquire. At the same time, people in their twenties are striving to succeed genetically—to reproduce. They have to find a mate. They must have children and provide for them.

At some point in a person's thirties, though, perspective changes. There may still be promotions in store, but they will be less frequent and less urgently needed. Partnership is either secured or not going to happen. Marriage and the birth of children are in the past. The house is bought and the cars are in the garage. What do we strive for now? For some the answer is a bigger house and more cars to put in its garage. For some the answer is a lower handicap.

We could, of course, strive to make the world around us better. We could work harder on loving our families. We could feed the hungry and tutor the illiterate and build shelter for the homeless.

But, Rotella told me, that would still leave us with a need to play.

Some of us have devalued the word "play." It's something we tell little children to run outside and do when we want to be free of them for a while. Rotella took play very seriously. His views were rooted in his religious upbringing in Vermont. We are all endowed, he believed, with certain talents and abilities. Some are physical; some are mental. Our purpose in this world is to make the fullest possible use of all of them.

The trouble is that our culture has divided most of our activities into two categories, the mental and the physical. If you work with your mind, your body is an encumbrance, a piece of flesh slowly dying in a chair. If you work with your body, your mind is often superfluous. Ford doesn't really want you to think too much about the seats you're installing in the new Taurus. Just do it. Check your will and your dreams at the gate.

It's only in certain kinds of play—and most especially in golf—that most of us find opportunities to engage both body and mind, to integrate our abilities, to be fully ourselves. And that, Rotella believed, is why golf fascinates and even obsesses us. When we play golf, we are being our best selves. Our bodies and our minds are both fully engaged. We are doing what we are here to do.

I found that there were times on the golf course when this was easier to grasp than at other times. I did not, for instance, sense an ultimate purpose on that ugly afternoon when my pathetic wedge ricocheted off the cart bridge and nearly took out Rotella's eye. But there were other moments. They were not necessarily moments of great scoring or great shots. Sometimes they occurred when I was struggling just to keep the ball on the golf course. In the intensity of such moments, I understood that Rotella was right in believing that the beauty of golf lay in the way that it engaged all the faculties, body and mind.

But even understanding that, I knew there were other layers to explore and that I might never get to the kernel of the *matryoshka* that was the interplay between golf and the mind.

The Playing Field as Art

Eighteen dramas, some tragical, some farcical, in every round.

—Haultain

Of the factors that distinguish golf from other sports, the most obvious is the ground on which it is played. Tennis, football, basketball, even baseball—in all of these, the arena is more or less standard. Much is made in tennis of the distinction between grass and clay surfaces, or in baseball of the difference between left field in Fenway Park and left field in Yankee Stadium. But these differences are trivial in comparison to the variety offered by even the most rudimentary golf course.

A golf course is eighteen different arenas, spread out over perhaps one hundred acres of land. It usually encompasses fields and streams, woodlands and dells, hillsides and valleys. Within each hole is an all but inexhaustible array of challenges, changing daily with the wind and weather. And within the world of golf, there are many thousands of unique courses.

Somewhere in all that variety, there may be a course so dull and ugly as to be not worth playing. If so, I have yet to find it. I've been fortunate enough to play on some of the most celebrated courses in the world. I've played on some of the humblest munis. I've liked them all. This appeal stems from more, obviously, than a gene that predisposes me to like clipped grasslands. If it were only that, I could as happily have taken up sheepherding as golf.

As I considered the contribution that the golf course itself makes to the pleasure of the game, I realized that my tastes were untutored. When I played a course, I responded to some of its most superficial aspects. Was it pretty? Was the grass thick and sturdy and green? Did it give the feeling that an orderly mind had shaped nature without destroying it? And, not least, was it fun to play? Were its holes ones that an average player could at least hope to par, or did it bludgeon a player like me with a succession of long, difficult holes he could only par by getting improbably lucky?

These did not strike me as unreasonable standards to apply to a golf course. But there was obviously more to learn about why some courses were more pleasurable than others. It seemed a good idea to talk to someone who designed them. I had heard of a golf architect named Tom Doak; he'd written a couple of books on golf courses. When I saw an item in a local golf magazine that said he was designing a new course in my area, I looked up his office number and gave him a call. He invited me to meet him.

The course was in the Norfolk area. It was called, then, Harbour View, though its name would be changed before it opened for play. I found it, following his directions, just over the bridge-tunnel that carries Interstate 664 over the James River at Hampton Roads. The ground was low, flat, brown, and in late autumn, muddy. The James formed one boundary of the peninsula on which it lay. The Nansemond, a broad tidal estuary, formed another. Fingers of swampy, cattailed marsh spread through the property. Ragged clumps of shedding trees dotted the horizon. It was not the sort of land I would have driven by and thought, "This would make a great golf course."

Doak met me in the developer's office, which occupied a one-story brick house that seemed likely to have been, until recently, a farmer's home. Though he was thirty-six, he looked much younger, with lank brown hair that hung over his forehead, brown eyes, and the kind of goatee that a college freshman might grow. He wore jeans, a golf shirt, a Gore-Tex jacket, and muddy hiking boots.

We got into his rental car to take a look at the golf course layout, and as we drove, I asked him how he'd gotten started in golf.

"My Dad's not a big golfer and never has been," Doak said. "When I was growing up, we weren't members of a club. But a few times a year, he'd go to a processors' convention to meet with the people he did business with over the phone—he bought corn oil and soybean oil and commodities like that for Lever Brothers. These processors had good taste in convention sites—they were usually golf resorts. Dad would take the family. The first course I ever saw was Sea Pines, down at Hilton Head, South Carolina. Then Harbor Town.

"Harbor Town was new then, and it had gotten a lot of acclaim. Charles Price, the golf writer, lived down there, and he'd spent a lot of time with Pete Dye when Pete was designing it. When it was done, he'd written a little booklet, kind of like the yardage book you'd see today, but without the yardages. It had a diagram of each hole and a paragraph about the design and how you might play it. For instance, he'd say you might want to drive to the left side of the fairway on No. 2, because from the right side your approach might be blocked by trees. That was the first thing I'd read about course architecture. It was very simple, it made sense, and it was interesting."

Doak remembered a feeling of comfort and ease that came over him the first time he saw a golf course, at the age of ten. He was not sure why he'd felt that way. But golf quickly became his passion. He liked to play, of course. But he was also fascinated from the beginning by the design of golf courses.

"By the time I was fourteen, I pretty much had the *World Atlas of Golf* memorized," he recalled.

He went to Cornell (I seemed to be running into lots of people with Cornell backgrounds) intending to be a golf course architect. It was not something the university offered as a field of study. Doak fashioned his own major on an informal basis. He learned a lot on his own by the simple expedient of writing to the managers of famous golf courses and asking if he could visit them and, if not play, at least walk them. Many of them were private courses. But Doak was persistent, and he was perhaps the only college student back then sending neatly typed letters to golf clubs expressing a polite desire to have a look around. He talked his way through a lot of gates.

"I had to write several letters to get to see Pine Valley," he recalled. "Ernie Ransome—he's not the president there anymore but he pretty much runs the place—wrote back and said, 'Sorry, guests may only play with a member.' I wrote back and said I know you have to play with a member but I'm really interested in architecture and I'd like to come. He wrote back and said that was nice but you still have to play with a member. So I wrote back again and said, 'Well, you're a member, aren't you?'

"So he was nice enough to invite me. Turned out he wasn't there when I came. But he had the manager take care of me, and I played the course with the guy who's the pro there now. And they didn't just hustle me in and out. They let me spend all day there, visit with the superintendent, visit the library. So I got a really good look at the place."

By the time he finished Cornell, studying golf courses had become Doak's passion. He got to them in an old Mustang II that he wore out in three years. He never passed up a chance to see a course that promised to teach him something. He recalled that at the end of his senior year, he skipped the pregraduation parties to drive to Crystal Downs, an all-but-forgotten Alister MacKenzie course he'd heard about in upper Michigan, and then spent a couple of days at the Memorial Tournament, outside Columbus, Ohio, having a look at Jack Nicklaus's Muirfield Village course.

He wangled a grant from Cornell for a year of study abroad and moved to St. Andrews, the university town on the North Sea coast of Scotland where golf was, if not born, at least developed into the game we know.

"I wanted to work on the grounds crew at St. Andrews, but that didn't work out because their unemployment rate then was like twenty percent and they couldn't justify hiring an American kid instead of a local kid on the crew," Doak recalled as the car turned toward a long strip of brown earth. I could see lines of small plastic red and yellow flags stuck in the ground.

Instead, the caddie master at St. Andrews took Doak on as a kind of second-class looper. He was not permitted to take work away from the career caddies. But when they had all gotten out for the morning, Doak would be given a bag to carry. Quite often his clients were Japanese tourists whom the Scottish caddies disdained—not because they were poor tippers but because many of them had only rarely been able to play golf on the limited number of courses in their own country.

"I caddied for one or two who I don't think had ever played a full round of golf in their lives," Doak recalled. "They'd learned golf on a driving range, but that was all. I remember I had to line one guy up about thirty degrees left of where I wanted him to go, he cut across the ball so badly.

"But that was great experience. And I also eventually got to go out with some better players, members of the Royal & Ancient Golf Club, and so on. The Old Course at St. Andrews is the most complicated strategic course in the world, bar none. You can learn it in two ways. You can play it so often that you see it in all the varying wind conditions, and you see how bunkers only one hundred and fifty yards from the tee are in play one day and bunkers two hundred and ninety

yards off the tee are in play the next. Or you learn it by caddying for people, some of whom can hit it only one hundred
and forty yards. In two months' caddying at the Old Course,
I got to know it pretty well."

When he'd spent enough time in St. Andrews, Doak began
to travel. He saw all the famed Scottish courses and a lot that
were unknown to all but their neighbors. "I saw one hundred
and seventy golf courses in that year," Doak said. "I had a list of
about a hundred I wanted to see, and then I'd ask what else was
in the area that was worth playing and seeing. I went to some
courses because I heard they had one or two interesting holes."

We got out of the car and started walking along the muddy
ground that would someday be Harbour View's eighth hole, a
short par five with trees and marsh along the right side and a
street of new suburban homes along the left. Doak and an assistant were placing marking flags to show the contractor
where to plant the various grasses—Bermuda in the fairways
and rougher fescues in the fringe areas.

I asked Doak about the main impressions he'd gleaned
from Scottish golf courses. "The most interesting thing to me
was the variety of shots you'd play over there as opposed to
here. A putt from thirty yards off the green—that might be
the thing to do. You might be one hundred and forty yards
from a green and have to take a three-iron and let it roll up
rather than try to hit it through the air. The bunkers were really deep, and sometimes you'd have to play sideways just to
get out. You nearly always played in the wind, blowing from
every angle you can think of. People in the United States, especially Tour players, have learned to play one way. They
might play a fade and they hit the same fade everywhere. The
conditions don't usually get so tough that a fade won't work.
In Britain sooner or later you're going to come up against a
hole where you cannot play your normal game. If you get a
wind quartering from the left at forty miles an hour, that fade
may wind up ninety yards in the wrong direction. So it en-
courages you to learn to do other things."

I could imagine, suddenly, the eighth at Harbour View playing in such a wind. Just about any shot I'd care to hit from the tee, save a putt, would be likely to end up in the marsh. A low, on-command draw is not part of my repertoire.

The green on No. 8 hove into view, a vaguely elliptical shape of sculpted sand and gravel, ready for seeding. Doak was still talking animatedly about Scottish golf courses.

"Most of the courses there are entirely natural. The bunkers were built by some guy with a shovel in a couple of days. And they were really good golf courses! They didn't spend a lot on conditioning [the turf]. There are some courses where you can barely tell where the fairway ends and the rough begins. At certain times of the year, with no irrigation systems back then, all the grass got burned out and you couldn't tell at all. You just had to figure out where between here and the hole you wanted to hit the ball. At St. Andrews the fairway is usually shared by a hole going out and one coming in, and there are bunkers in the middle. So you couldn't just aim down the fairway and hit away."

He recollected the twelfth hole at St. Andrews in particular. It was a short par four, little more than three hundred yards. But there were a half-dozen possible ways to play it, depending on the wind and the pin position in the huge green that the hole shared with the sixth hole. A player had to decide where to place his drive, depending on which bunkers the day's wind put in play. Then he had to decide whether to pitch the ball onto the green or run it up, depending again on the wind and on where the flag was set.

To Doak the validation of No. 12's greatness was the fact that it gave problems to great players despite its modest length. "A lot of guys have screwed it up," he recalled. "Watson bogeyed it when he lost the Open there. It's always been a tough hole for good players."

When Doak returned to the United States from this year of study abroad, he went to work for the man whose work at

Harbor Town had first kindled his desire to build golf courses, Pete Dye. As a profession, golf architecture has two primary points of access. A would-be architect can establish himself as a player, the way Nicklaus, Palmer, Tom Weiskopf, and others have done. Or he can serve an apprenticeship with an established architect. That was Doak's route, though it was not an apprenticeship in any formal sense. Pete Dye did not, Doak said, try to pass along his ideas about course design. In fact, he disliked being asked why he planned a particular hole in a particular way. But there were many opportunities to watch and learn, times when Dye would grab a stick and start drawing alternative routes for golf holes in the dirt, and Doak could see the thinking that went into each choice.

Doak spent a couple of years as a construction worker for Dye, learning to operate a bulldozer and sculpt land, learning the nuts and bolts of course construction. Eventually Dye moved him into the office and let him start helping on course plans, but it was not an entirely comfortable relationship. "I bugged him," Doak recalled, "because I asked too many questions."

Before he turned thirty, Doak set out on his own. He formed a company called Renaissance Golf. It was so named, he said, because he wanted everyone in the company to be a "Renaissance man" of golf course construction, a man equally capable of running a bulldozer and plotting drainage patterns and conceiving the perfect route for a short, tricky par five. And he wanted to emphasize his determination to design courses that drew on the traditions of golf architecture's classical period, much as the Italian Renaissance drew on the traditions of Greece and Rome.

I thought the name was appropriate for a couple of additional reasons. First, Doak had trained himself for his profession in much the way that artists trained themselves in the Renaissance, by carefully studying the classics and then apprenticing himself to a master. And second, Doak and his company worked in much the same way as did the ateliers of

Renaissance painters. They depended, as the Renaissance artists did, on commissions from people of means—in this case, the means to buy the land and pay for the construction of a course. Just as Leonardo did no spec frescoes, golf course architects did not plan or build a course and then look for someone to buy it. And their product was a group effort. Doak did the overall design and sometimes immersed himself in the details. But he gave a lot of latitude to the experienced members of his staff, letting them decide on the shape and look of a particular bunker or green—much as the Renaissance artists often painted the main figures in a picture and let their assistants fill in the background.

In going off on his own, Doak was bucking a trend in golf course architecture in favor of professional players with big names. This was not a completely new phenomenon. A hundred years ago Harry Vardon was writing that only a first-class player could design a good golf course because only he would know how to make a course sufficiently testing to distinguish the true expert from the merely decent player. This was like saying that only a great musician could compose music. The truth is that an architect must be familiar with the capabilities of great players just as a composer must know the limits of musicians' capabilities; he doesn't necessarily have to have them. But as Doak got started, it began to seem as if every player on the PGA Tour who'd won a major championship was following Nicklaus and Palmer into the course design business. Besides whatever skill and imagination they brought to it, such players had marquee value. A Jack Nicklaus "signature course" added perceptible value to the development lots that generally surrounded it. A course by Renaissance Golf didn't have the same immediate impact on the bottom line. Nicklaus has done dozens of courses in the past twenty years. Doak, who has a handicap of about seven when he's playing regularly, had designed about ten courses when I met him.

He had developed a reputation as a "minimalist" architect,

a designer who did relatively little to the land he was given. This was in part due to his belief that the best American courses, the classics, were designed before World War II by architects like Alister MacKenzie and Donald Ross. They had only mule-drawn scrapers to shape the land, so they worked with the terrain they were given. Massive earth-moving equipment was a by-product of World War II; the Seabees had developed bulldozers to construct airfields. Postwar architects took advantage of the new technology to move huge amounts of dirt, imposing their ideas on the terrain. Sometimes they had no choice but to do so. They were not given pieces of land of the same caliber as MacKenzie and Ross had worked with. Nevertheless, they often produced holes that looked artificial. Doak did not think their courses generally justified the expense and upheaval. (Neither do a lot of other people. The most important rotating American championship, the U.S. Open, is nearly always played on courses that date from the classic period.) Doak used bulldozers in his work, mules and scrapers being hard to come by. But he tended to leave the terrain much as he'd found it. He told me his goal was to make his greens look not as if an architect had created them, but as if they had always been there.

We walked from the eighth green area toward the tee for the fifth hole, which was across the road. I asked Doak what he would say if someone who knew nothing about golf or golf courses asked him why an architect was necessary. What was the architect's prime task?

We stepped out onto the future fifth tee, a flattened piece of ground that overlooked a finger of marsh perhaps sixty yards across. Ahead of us I could see a single massive oak tree standing like a sentinel on the bank across the marsh. Beyond it was the brown gash through the woods where the land had been cleared for a fairway.

"The first thing an architect has to do is an engineering problem, the route of the course," Doak said in response to my question.

The architect has to look at a tract of land and define eighteen holes. He has to make certain they'll drain, that their par will add up to a number between 70 and 72, that there will be some par threes and some par fives, and that the overall length will be somewhere around seven thousand yards. This isn't a simple problem. There are an infinite number of possible courses in a large tract of land. And the architect usually doesn't get to pick a route based solely on his esthetic judgments. He has to negotiate with the owner of the property, who quite often wants prime sites left for housing, and with government environmental officials, who quite often don't want golf holes impinging on areas they consider sensitive. When Doak submitted his first routing for Harbour View, it came back with all but one hole rejected.

But the solution to the engineering problem, while essential, was only the first step for a good architect. The more important step, he said, was to make the course interesting. That was where engineering ended and art began.

What, I asked, made it interesting?

"Partly, it's the way the hole looks," Doak said. "It's visual intimidation. Does it look scary in some way? MacKenzie said his goal was to make golf look harder than it really was. You want to make it look hard enough so that the golfer feels he's accomplished something if he hits a good shot. But you can't make it so hard that the course punishes the golfer all day and he shoots a million."

What else made a hole interesting?

"It's the element of strategy and choice," Doak said. "You try to arrange it so that on every shot the golfer has some strategy to plan and choices to make and risks to run. You can't always do that. But that's the ideal."

Risk was a fundamental factor in the greatness of courses like St. Andrews, Doak believed. Once a golfer learned the Old Course, he weighed risks on every shot. When he hit a tee shot, he knew where the Old Course bunkers were, including the hidden ones. He knew how hard they could be

to escape. He knew how quickly a putt too boldly str
could slide down into a hollow on a St. Andrews green and
turn a potential birdie into a bogey. He knew how small the
difference could be between a great shot and a disastrous one,
a shot that ended up trapped in the Beardies or safe in the
Elysian Fields. A drive over the sheds on the Road Hole, for
instance, could be brilliant if it drew into the fairway. If it
didn't draw quite enough, it could fall out of bounds, costing
a severe penalty.

Good golf holes, Doak believed, were holes like the ones at
St. Andrews that confronted a golfer with strategic choices
and risks. Weighing the risks and running some of them gave
the game a constant frisson of foreboding and adrenaline, of
nervous tension, of triumphant satisfaction. That was one of
the reasons why the golf course, properly designed, made the
game so enjoyable and so distinguished from other sports.

I could see some of those elements in the future fifth hole,
even though it was as yet just a crescent-shaped swath
through the woods with a couple of dimples in the land
where bunkers would someday be. The element of visual intimidation began with the fact that the tee shot had to clear
about sixty yards of marsh to reach the fairway. It was an insignificant carry to any average player, and Doak had a
shorter tee penciled in for the other side of the marsh for
players whose strength was well below average. But who
hasn't topped a ball off a tee? If I were playing Harbour View's
fifth, I'd notice the marsh before I hit my tee shot. I probably
wouldn't hit a ball into it, but I'd notice it.

The sentinel oak provided another source of visual intimidation and an element of risk. There was plenty of room to
the right of the tree. But avoiding it would give a golfer
something else to think about as he stood on the tee. If he
pushed the ball too far to the right, he risked slicing it into
the woods that lined the right side of the hole.

The fifth would be a short par four, three hundred and
fifty-three yards. It would be a dogleg to the left, with a

bunker at the corner of the fairway on the right side and another bunker guarding the left side of the green. The green itself tilted fairly sharply from left to right. It seemed at first a simple, unremarkable design, but as Doak explained it, it began to look more complex.

To begin with, the fifth adhered to something Doak had learned from Pete Dye. Dye, Doak said, believed in avoiding four hundred–yard par fours when he designed holes. They were too long for the average golfer and not long enough to challenge the expert. It was better, he believed, to design par fours that were either quite long or quite short. The long holes would challenge the expert player, even though the average player would probably be well advised to regard them as par fives, reachable in three shots instead of two. And the short holes, if well conceived, would be challenging for the expert, especially if he wanted to make a birdie, and at the same time playable for the average golfer seeking par. The fifth fell squarely into the short par four class.

The design elements that would make the fifth interesting for all types of golfers, Doak said, were the oak tree, the shape of the fairway, the two bunkers, and the tilt of the green. The oak tree was intended to cut off the player tempted to blast his tee shot directly toward the green. (That was important not only for strategic purposes but because Doak knew the developer intended to sell housing lots along the left side of the hole. He wanted to design the hole in such a way that future backyards were far from the intended landing area for tee shots.) The bunker to the left of the green and the tilt of the green were also intended to nudge the player to the right. Especially if a pin were cut close to the bunker, a shot from the left side of the fairway would become very delicate. In order to get close to the pin, it would have to clear the bunker and stop on a downslope.

Doak meant for an intelligent player to realize that the smarter strategy was to play down the right side of the fairway, risking the fairway bunker. If such a shot went the right distance in the right direction, it would be rewarded with a somewhat easier approach to the green. This approach would not have to clear the greenside bunker. It would have a better chance of stopping close to the pin.

Doak hoped that good players would decide to risk hitting their drivers off the tee on No. 5, trying to get into position for this open approach and a chance to make birdie. Of course, the approach shot then would probably be less than a full wedge shot, testing the expert's ability to modulate his pitches to a precise distance.

Average players, meanwhile, would have other decisions to make and risks to weigh in their quest for a par. For them the fairway bunker, two-hundred-and-twenty yards or so from the tee, would be a more threatening element in the hole than it would for the expert. For one thing, average players tend to slice, and the bunker was on the right side. For another, average players have difficulty picking a ball cleanly from a trap when they have to hit a long shot. An expert could probably count on hitting a one-hundred-and-twenty-yard pitch from the bunker to the green three times out of four. For the average player the ratio would more likely be one time in five. So he would have to decide whether to use his driver off the tee and risk hitting the bunker, or lay up short with another club and make his approach shot longer.

We crossed the marsh on a bridge made of board that was new and pale, unweathered. We walked toward the future green. I could see from the way that the sand was shaped that it would have a pronounced tilt and a lot of humps and swales. Doak said he tried to design greens so that the hole would play differently from day to day. On some days, perhaps most, a standard high pitch would be the best shot to play into No. 5. But occasionally, from certain spots in the fairway to certain pin positions atop shelves and knobs in the green near the edge of the bunker, it might be better to try to play a low shot that landed in front of the green and rolled up. Doak wanted to give the player options because options added interest.

We made our way from the fifth green to another bridge, spanning a more substantial portion of marsh. Doak wanted to check on the work being done on a portion of the course's future back nine. He talked for a while with Eric Iverson, his bulldozer operator. Iverson was working on the bunkering for the sixteenth hole, trying to add visual and strategic interest to a hole that would cover uninteresting land, a flat former soybean field. He and Doak used the bulldozer on the land as an artist uses a pencil on sketch paper. They gouged a bunker and a lip out of the ground. Doak decided it was too high. Iverson erased it with the bulldozer blade and gouged another one. Eventually Doak was satisfied and we moved on.

We emerged from some woods to find a large abandoned quarry full of water, perhaps two hundred yards in diameter. This was the source for a lot of the stone and gravel that had gone into the construction of Interstate 664. It was about as ugly as a body of water can be, with bare, muddy brown banks and a couple of dirt service roads left over from the quarrying operation. Trunk power lines traversed the property overhead.

Doak was building a par four hole around the circumference of this old quarry. No. 12 at Harbour View would begin from tees set low along the bank. The golfer would see the water to his right all the way to the hole, which would be four hundred and sixty yards from the back tee and four hundred and thirty-eight yards from the tees most players would use. Immediately in front of him would be a long waste bunker serving as a kind of beach and running perhaps one hundred and eighty yards out from the tee. The fairway was one of the few at Harbour View for which Doak planned to alter substantially the natural terrain. It would have two levels, the upper one being farther from the water. An enormous, high-lipped bunker was taking shape thirty yards in front of the green, which was situated around a slight bend in the quarry.

It was not, I thought, the sort of hole I looked forward to

playing. It seemed too hard for the average player and his tendency to slice. The average golfer would have to hit two superb shots just to get close to the green. I could imagine an enormous number of balls sliced into the quarry by players swinging too hard.

When I mentioned this to Doak, he was not apologetic. "Golf is supposed to be hard," he said. "Every course should have some tough holes."

Doak pointed out that by creating a broad fairway with two levels, he was giving the average player options. He could choose to aim well left of the water with his drive and reach the upper level. Attacked this way, the hole would be longer but safer. He could then play a second shot along the upper level and leave himself a short pitch to the green. He would be surrendering to the hole in a sense, conceding that he would not make par, at least not by the standard procedure of hitting the green with the second shot. But he would probably make a bogey this way.

I asked Doak what audience he had in mind when he designed a course. Was it the average player? The average male golfer's handicap, according to the USGA, is about sixteen strokes, suggesting that his normal score is around 90. And that covers just those golfers who maintain handicaps, themselves a small minority of the total golfing population. The true average score is probably closer to 105 than 90.

Or was he designing for the expert? Golf tradition favored the expert. Vardon had written that a well-designed course was one that required some shots the average player couldn't hit. That was how it assured that the best players would emerge victorious. In Vardon's view, courses needed penal bunkers stretching from one side of the fairway to another at a sufficient distance from the tee so that only good players could clear them.

The courses of the classic period had softened this contemptuous attitude toward mediocre golfers. Ross, designing for resort guests at Pinehurst, had taken pride in building courses that players of all abilities could play and enjoy while at the same time giving the expert a chance to demonstrate his superiority.

Doak replied that he, like Ross, tried to design for both audiences. The principal developer at Harbour View was an excellent golfer, a four-handicapper who belonged to clubs like Butler National and Pine Valley. He wanted a course he could proudly invite his equally adept friends to play. At the same time Doak was hearing from others in the company who wanted him to make sure the course was enjoyable for the home buyers and daily-fee players they wanted to attract. And obviously Doak had his own notions of what makes a first-class golf course.

Doak's answer to these conflicting pressures was to build four tees on each hole so that the course played from as many as six thousand, seven hundred yards to as few as five thousand, two hundred. He designed broad fairways and tried to put most of the course's hazards and difficulties around the greens. He tried to be accommodating of the average player's length or lack of it. The closing hole at Harbour View, for instance, would be a par five with a marsh running across the entire breadth of the fairway. Good players would be able to clear the marsh with their second shots, setting up a short pitch to the green. Excellent players would be going for the green in two shots. But Doak did not want to deprive the player who couldn't clear the marsh in two strokes of a chance to make par. He fiddled with the placement of the green until he had it arranged so that a player who hit a poor drive could lay up short of the marsh and still be only one-hundred-and-eighty yards from the hole, leaving him at least the possibility of recovering and saving par with an excellent third shot.

But beyond a certain point, his sympathy for the average player gave way to his desire to challenge the expert. He felt that the average player would not get a lot of satisfaction from the occasional routine pars that might come his way on Harbour View's easier holes. But if he managed to par a tough hole like No. 12, he would cherish that memory for a while.

I asked Doak to stay in touch about Harbour View's progress and to let me know when I could see the finished product. Fifteen months later he called to let me know that the course was almost ready. He would be visiting to check on the final preparations and to take some photographs. I invited myself to tag along.

A year's time had wrought evident changes. Road construction crews were busy paving the last stretch of a four-lane boulevard to carry traffic through the development. There were more houses, and a few of them, judging by the bicycles and basketball goals in the driveways, had families living in them. The golf course had recently been sold to a company called Links Corporation. The course's name had been changed to Riverfront at Harbour View. It was a month away from opening for public play. But it was already green and inviting, sparkling in the sun.

I found Doak out by the tenth tee, on the corner of a broad, flat piece of land that would someday hold parking lots and a clubhouse. He was wearing shorts, hiking boots, and a replica baseball hat from the old New York Cubans of the Negro Leagues. His goatee was gone, and his face reflected a quiet happiness. He'd been out playing holes on the golf course. He was like a vintner after opening the first bottles of wine from a good harvest. The satisfaction was all the sweeter because of his role in creating it.

The course itself was not quite finished. The greens, which had been seeded first, were in excellent condition, velvety and smooth. The fairways still had some rough patches where drainage problems had caused seed to wash away. But their Bermuda cloak was for the most part lush and thick. In a lot of places around the edges of the course, scars made by earthmoving equipment remained. The course reminded me of a teenager who's reached his full height but still needs to outgrow the pimply stage. The handsome, mature adult is foreseeable but not quite there yet.

We walked over to the first tee. I felt for a moment what it might be like to realize the fantasy of owning one's own golf course, with no starter, no pro shop, no waiting for tee times, no slow foursomes clogging the fairways ahead. We could play whenever we were ready.

Doak suggested we play No. 1 from the back tee, which stretched it to four hundred and twenty yards. The fairway was broad, lined by woods down the right side. But there was a bit of marsh in front of the tee and a large bunker shaped like an elongated amoeba in what seemed to be the perfect direction to aim a drive.

"Visual intimidation?" I asked.

"Yep," he said. "It's only about one-sixty to carry that bunker."

I aimed over the bunker's right edge and hit a low drive that nevertheless cleared it easily and skipped down the fairway. I was reminded of what Doak had said about designing a course so that players got a feeling of accomplishment from merely decent shots.

I hit a four-iron approach and pushed it, winding up in a bunker. As I walked toward the green, I remembered what he had told me about designing them so that they looked as if they'd always been there. As far as I could tell, he'd succeeded. The first green had a lot of slopes and undulations. But it looked as if the wind had sculpted its contours over centuries' time, not like something created with a bulldozer a year and a half earlier. I hit a decent explosion and left myself a ten-foot putt. Lining it up, I couldn't tell if it would break a few inches to the right or not. Doak looked the putt over also and then pointed out the drainage pattern on the green. Putts tended to go the way the water drained, he said, and this one would probably break a couple of inches to the right. I lined it up and hit it. It went dead straight, missing the hole by a couple of inches on the left.

Doak shrugged, grinned. He did not look displeased that his creation had fooled us both.

We walked over to the second tee. We faced a par three, about one hundred and eighty yards from the middle tee. Doak hit an iron and did not hit it well, catching turf before he hit the ball. His shot carried only about one hundred and twenty yards and was pulled left, into a bunker. My own four-iron shot was too good. It flew the green and settled in another bunker.

I could not restrain a feeling of *Schadenfreude* over what had befallen Doak. I have always felt that bunkers placed fifty or sixty yards away from greens are a sadistic element in any golf course. They rarely bother the good player. But they make life miserable for the hacker, who's got enough trouble without having to execute a long explosion, one of the toughest shots in golf.

I was impolitic enough to express this thought to Doak. He disagreed. "If you don't have that bunker there, it means the shot for someone who doesn't reach the green is just dull," he said. "I don't think it's asking too much for him to at least miss to one side."

But the long bunker shot bedeviled him. He caught too much ball and hit over the green, stopping just short of a stretch of tall, marshy grass in which the ball would have been lost. He made five on the hole. So did I, after a weak bunker shot and a three-putt caused by misreading a hump Doak had built into the green and hitting my first putt well past the hole.

It was the sort of early adversity that can sometimes spoil a round of golf, making the player pity himself. But Doak's thinking was starting to affect my own. These humps and bunkers, I thought, were not unfair. They provided the challenges golf courses needed to have. They enriched the game.

On the third tee Doak was apologetic. A road planned by

the developer had affected the length of this hole, he said. He'd intended it to be a par five. But he'd had to shorten it, and the result was a long par four, four hundred and sixty yards, with marsh guarding the right side of the green.

Our drives, into a slight breeze, left us each well over two hundred yards to go. I took a seven-iron and pitched down the fairway toward the post in the ground marking one hundred yards to the middle of the green. Doak took a three-wood and went for it. His ball, cut slightly, disappeared into the marsh.

It was, again, a moment tinged with *Schadenfreude.* Didn't he think, I asked, that four hundred and sixty yards was a little long for a par four for average players? I had always felt that way.

Doak disagreed. He said it didn't matter much to him whether the hole was designated a par four or a par five, and in fact the course's owners were thinking of reversing the usual placement of the experts' blue tees and average players' white tees, setting it up as a four-hundred-seventy-five-yard par five from the white tees and a four-hundred-sixty-yard par four from the blues.

The hole presented certain strategic options regardless of what the scorecard said par should be, he explained. It could be played conservatively, as I had done, with five the likely outcome. Or it could be played boldly by someone trying to make four and willing to risk a six or a seven. The same player might make different decisions on different days, depending on the wind and the way he'd hit the ball on the first two holes. That was what made it interesting.

We explored further. I flunked the test Doak had prepared at the fifth hole, pushing my drive into the lone fairway bunker. I decided that I should have hit a three-wood off the tee. Most of the holes, I found, were of manageable length, and with Doak along, I was more aware than usual of the ways in which the design required a player to think. My approach to the seventh green was typical. I pulled it a bit left and the ball hit a side slope. It rolled down into a closely mowed hollow six feet from the putting surface. I looked up at the pin and found I had at least three options. I could putt the ball, trying to gauge how much the slightly longer grass on the fringe of the green and the subsequent slope would affect the distance it would roll. I could chip into the slope. Or I could lob over the slope. I tried all three options. I found that the standard play from six feet off the green, the chip, which I probably would have tried in a competitive round, worked worst. The chipped ball was the only one of the three I failed to get up and down.

It was an elegantly designed green, reminiscent of the greens Ross designed at Pinehurst. Doak smiled when I told him this. In fact, he said, he'd designed this green along the lines of the right half of the double green on No. 12 at St. Andrews.

"The key to interesting greens is the variety of shots you get around them," he said. "It's a cliché, but everyone has a tendency to design courses to fit his own game, including me. I have a good short game, because when I was a kid, I wasn't able to hit the ball very far. So my courses have more than the average amount of difficulty around the greens. I'm a little wild off the tee, so my courses tend to have wide fairways."

They did. The fairways, as they were being cut then, were generally at least fifty yards wide. This spaciousness accomplished several things. It would tend to keep play moving, of course, because players would have to look for fewer lost balls. It would tend to make even poor players feel that the course gave them a chance. And I found that it had a beneficial effect on my swing. Relieved of concern about encroaching woodlands or rough, I started to loosen up. As we played the back nine, I began hitting the ball as well as I had in several months. Contact got crisper. Distance improved. I even reached the long twelfth hole with a well-struck three-wood, though I proceeded to three-putt the large green.

As we played the final few holes, my appreciation of the course grew. Riverfront at Harbour View was not destined to be famous. The PGA Tour was not going to stop there, and the USGA was not going to consider it for an Open championship. It was going to be just one of many new daily-fee courses in the United States serving average players in its neighborhood. But it would have been wrong to call it ordinary. Too much thought, too much skill, too much devotion had gone into each of its holes. It was, in its own way, a work of art. So are thousands of other golf courses.

As it happened, I birdied the eighteenth hole. As Doak had intended, the hole made me feel I had accomplished something special simply by hitting decent shots. My drive found the big fairway. My second shot cleared the marsh. I chipped onto the green with my third, banking the ball off a swale. I sank the putt from ten feet. I smiled when the ball slipped in, and not just because birdies are rare enough that I always smile when I make one. I smiled because I was thinking of all the pleasure that the golfers who came after me would get from this piece of artfully reworked ground.

The Mechanics

The thousand and one things that we should not do in golf are evidence of the difficulties of the game.

—Haultain

I know how important the swing is in golf. I have this from no less an authority than David Duval.

I met Duval about six months before he broke through to win his first professional tournament, starting a tear that would take him to the top of the world rankings. As I mentioned, Bob Rotella had asked me to fly to Phoenix, where he was working with Tour players at the Phoenix Open. He suggested that we meet at a California Pizza Kitchen across the road from his motel in Scottsdale, just after the dinner hour. When I arrived, he was finishing a meal with Duval.

Rotella introduced us, and we walked across the road to the motel parking lot, where both Duval and I were parked. I opened the trunk of my rental car to pull out my briefcase and computer. Duval glanced inside and saw my golf clubs. (Of course I'd brought them to Phoenix. Boy Scouts aren't the only ones who believe in being prepared.)

"Titleist DCIs," Duval observed. "Same clubs I play."

"The same?" I asked.

Duval nodded pleasantly. "Yeah."

I was skeptical. "You mean your clubs don't have some special super-stiff, custom-made shafts available only to pros? The clubheads aren't made of some special alloy? They're just DCIs like the ones I bought?"

Duval could see where this was going, and a smile flickered over his normally stolid face.

"Yeah."

"So does that mean," I asked, "that when I'm watching you on TV and you're playing some two-hundred-and-twenty yard par three with a creek in front and the announcer says, 'Duval has chosen a five-iron,' the only reason you can get a five-iron there and I'd have to lay up with a wood is that your swing is that much better than mine?"

He nodded solemnly. "Afraid so."

I was afraid of that too.

The golf swing has to be ranked among the elements that make golf fascinating. As Dr. Lichtenberg pointed out, humans tend to want to master the movements of their bodies. The swing, like ballet, gives us a movement of infinite complexity to work on.

But to be honest, I wish that Duval were wrong and that the mechanics of hitting a golf ball were not quite so important. After all, I sometimes think, ninety-nine percent of a player's swing really doesn't matter. The only part of the swing that affects the ball is two inches' worth about three-fourths of the way through the motion, when the clubhead strikes the ball. The rest is incidental, like the flavor of soup the diva had before walking on stage to sing. If you could figure out how to swing a golf club the way Gene Kelly twirled a cane during a soft shoe number and yet make that club travel one hundred and twenty miles an hour on the proper plane through the hitting zone, that would do perfectly well. Golf history is full of successful players with what were considered ugly swings. As I write this, Allen Doyle has just won the PGA Seniors' Championship with a swing that looks like a hockey player's slap shot. (Not surprisingly, he once was a hockey player.) If he showed up anonymously for a lesson at the driving range down the road from my home, the pro there would tell him he had to start from scratch and learn the swing all over because he'd never break a hundred with that hideous motion.

I say all this knowing that my attitude about golf mechanics is a self-interested one, born of the fact that my mechanics aren't very good.

I sometimes feel that my swing and I are like the poor, hungry masses on the freezing streets of prerevolutionary St. Petersburg in *Dr. Zhivago*, gazing at the warm and well-fed revelers in an elite Russian supper club with a mixture of resentment and envy. Of the two, envy is the stronger emotion. We may speak of them disparagingly. But in truth we yearn to be one of the elite, to know its secrets, to have its easy facility, to speak its jargon.

If you doubt that there is a jargon, tune in the next time NBC telecasts a tournament and listen to Johnny Miller and Roger Maltbie. "Looks like he laid that club off, John," Roger will say. What does that mean, anyway? Does it mean that some player didn't have enough work for all fourteen of the clubs in his bag, so he sent one home until demand picked up?

"Yeah, Rog, and that caused him to come over the top," Johnny will reply.

"Come over the top?" I muse as I watch. Isn't that something the doughboys did in World War I when they left the trenches to push back the Boche?

I know, I know. "Laying the club off" refers to the direction of the shaft during the backswing, and "coming over the top" is a sin the hands commit at the start of the downswing. But despite all I've read, I still hear things that befuddle me whenever true golf swing savants speak. I still don't know, for instance, what the "double-cross" is. Gary McCord often refers to it. I know it's not the same double-cross that George Raft used to pull on Edward G. Robinson. And I believe it makes the ball go left. But I have no idea how to execute it or avoid it.

I strive fitfully to persuade myself that this doesn't matter, that the whole cult of mechanics doesn't matter, even though I acknowledge that the reason David Duval's clubface, in those critical two inches, is moving straighter and faster than mine has a lot to do with everything that happens during the rest of our respective swings. I just believe the game will be more fun if I don't dwell on it, much as I once decided that while I undoubtedly might be more attractive to women if I looked more like Robert Redford, my social life would be better if I didn't get too hung up about it.

One reason for this is a conversation I had with a woman named Alison Thietje, who has become the personal trainer to a number of successful pros, including Justin Leonard and Tom Watson. When she goes out on tour, she often watches her clients play in pro-ams. She watches their amateur partners try to imitate their swings. This is a little bit like watching your grandmother take her '89 Oldsmobile out on the track at Daytona and try to imitate Jeff Gordon. Grandma can try to do what Jeff does, but she and he are not really working with the same equipment. And the amateurs that Alison sees, try as they might, haven't got the flexibility, the timing, or the rhythm to duplicate a professional's swing. The most important piece of equipment they own, the body, is seriously flawed.

Another reason is what I learned from Bob Rotella. The greatest improvement I've ever made in my golf game occurred when I followed Rotella's advice to trust my swing on the course and spend most of my practice time on chipping, pitching, and putting. When I slid back into considering my swing a work in progress, into renewing the quest for the controlled, powerful draw I've wanted since I was twelve, my improvement slowed, stopped, and reversed itself.

But in this agnostic attitude toward the cult of the swing, I am, I suspect, a minority. All around me I see evidence that learning to swing properly is one of golf's attractions.

The monthly golf magazines, for instance, have found that their readers like nothing better than a cover story that promises new tips to cure the slice. Never mind that April's feature on getting rid of that pesky slice offers different advice than March's feature on the same subject and that May will bring still different advice. Some golfers never tire of reading about the swing and tinkering with theirs.

There's even a cottage industry in what are called training aids. The back pages of the magazines and some of the remote crannies of the Internet are the marketing tools of this industry, much as the inside back cover of Superman comic books was the sales venue of choice years ago for the purveyors of whoopee cushions, handshake shockers, and x-ray eyeglasses that promised intimate looks through the clothing of the budding beauties of the sixth grade.

Over the Internet this morning, the training aids for sale at www.shotsavers.com included:

- The Whippy Tempomaster, a clubhead on a flexible rod like a buggy whip. "Super-flexible shaft teaches Mechanics, Tempo and Timing." Only $129.00.

- The M-Brace. This looks like a black Velcro barrel. It keeps the right knee in the correct posture during the backswing. $39.50.

- The Swing Lock. This appears to be a plastic compass that clips onto the shaft of the club and helps the player check his backswing position so he'll always be able to find his best swing. A bargain at $9.95.

- The Power Release Belt. "The only training aid that is able to help both sides coordinate the timing of the body with the swinging of the arms." Prevents the dreaded chicken wing; looks like a gaudy version of the belts grade school safety patrolmen used to wear, except that it slips over the biceps as well as around the waist. $59.95.

- Greg Norman's Secret. A gauntlet-like black device that slips over the wrist and locks it into the proper position. Oddly enough, I've watched the Shark practice several times, and each time he must've left the Secret in his other helicopter, because he was never wearing it. $27.95.

I can imagine myself walking onto the practice range with my Whippy Tempomaster in hand, my M-Brace on my right leg, my Power Release Belt girding my torso, Greg Norman's Secret strengthening my left wrist. People would no doubt assume, justifiably, that I was a lost extra looking for the set of the new comedy *Monty Python Plays Golf.*

Yet I know that golf's mechanics can engage an intelligent person for a lifetime. I know it because I've taken lessons from two such people, Bob Toski and Paul Runyan. This, of course, was all in the interests of literature. Rotella helped arrange the lessons when we were working on a book about the best way to learn the game. Going to see Toski and Runyan was the golfing equivalent of Luke Skywalker journeying to Yoda's planet for an advanced seminar on the Force. You just can't get much closer to the source of wisdom about the golf swing.

Toski was the Tour's leading money winner back in 1954. He earned more glory than money with that title in those days, though, and he retired from the Tour to teach and raise a family in Florida. In fact, his teaching career had informally begun much earlier, when he was a ten-year-old caddie at a course in Northampton, Massachusetts, politely showing young ladies from Smith College that, contrary to their intuition, the best way to chip a ball up and onto a green was to hit down on it.

Toski had worked with Judy Rankin, Tom Kite, and other touring pros. He co-founded *Golf Digest's* schools. He teaches now at a luxurious grass-tee practice facility in the Miami area. You won't often find him on the tee line with the drive-in customers, however. He teaches by appointment under a live oak at the other end of the range. In the winter there is usually a retinue of spectators at his lessons. Vacationing golf teachers and aspiring pros watch him teach, trying to pick up his insights and methods.

Toski was a year or so past seventy when I met him, but very spry. He was small, almost fragile in appearance, with pale blue eyes and gray hair hidden by a big white cap of the sort that golfers will always associate with Ben Hogan. The lines etched into his face by the sun were kindly lines, and he looked like a retired priest out for some exercise—until he began teaching the golf swing. Toski's teaching method suggested what might have happened if Lenny Bruce had become a Marine Corps drill instructor. He was profane, sarcastic, in your face, funny, withering. He didn't care. He had things to teach, and he wanted to make sure he had your attention.

"The lower body shifts laterally, so the right shoulder—?" he might ask me as he tried to explain a movement to me. "Drops" was the answer I had to have.

"If the right shoulder goes down, the left must go—?"

"Up," I filled in.

Toski could lecture for hours like that about swing mechanics. Ask him about Tiger Woods's swing and he would tell you how Tiger demonstrated that Hogan had erred in writing that the downswing began with a movement of the left hip. It was the right knee that drove a good downswing, Toski said. Tiger's right knee action was the source of his power. I nodded. It sounded good to me.

But Toski, when teaching, preferred not to talk theory. He tried to teach swing feelings. (The title of one of his instructional books, written with Davis Love, Jr., is *How to Feel a Good Golf Swing*.) In one of the lessons I saw him give, he demonstrated to a young player how the weight should shift during the swing by taking a golf ball and dribbling it thirty yards out into the range, first with the left foot, then with the right, à la Diego Maradona.

When he saw me swing, he decided that chief among my problems was a weak left side. This allowed my right side to dominate, producing a swing that was equally capable of pulling the ball left or slicing it and sending it spinning right. It was one of the worst flaws to have because it didn't produce a consistent mistake. I couldn't compensate by aiming left and letting the ball fade toward the target. I might pull it even farther left.

Toski laid his hands on my shoulders and told me to feel as if my left shoulder were coming out from under my chin very rapidly during the downswing. Then he had one of his retinue prop a ball on a slightly slanted board, like a water ski ramp, so that I had to swing the driver upward to make contact.

The idea was to force me out of my bad habit, to give me no choice but to swing the correct way. This was how Toski himself had been taught. His older brother, Jack, was a teaching pro in western Massachusetts. As a young player, Toski, being small, had developed a very strong grip. It was too strong, in fact, for him to play well on the professional level. His brother tried to persuade Toski to change his grip, but Toski refused. So Jack took away his old tee club, a three-wood. He gave him a flat-faced driver. That was the only club he'd allow Toski to practice with. With his old grip and the new club, Toski could hit only low duck-hooks. There was a summer of tears and frustration, but Toski eventually changed his grip and learned to hold the club properly.

He had an evident pride in his knowledge of the golf swing, and I sensed an undercurrent of competitiveness with other gurus. There was a whiff of this when I made the mistake of saying I had been trying to take the club back with passive hands, to let the large muscles control it. Letting the large muscles control the club was one of the concepts propounded by David Leadbetter. It was as if I had whistled a Mozart air in the Salieri household. Toski did not like hearing the words *large* and *muscles* or *passive* and *hands* in the same sentences. His eyes flashed and his expression became withering.

"The club is connected to you by the—?" he demanded.

"Hands," I said sheepishly, like a scolded schoolboy.

"When you swing, the power comes through the—?"

"Hands," I repeated.

"I looked up the word *passive* in the dictionary, and it means lifeless and inert," he said. "Is that how your hands should be?"

"No," I confessed.

"Good," he nodded. "Golf starts with the hands and feet."

We went on.

Toski very quickly had me launching beautiful drives (by my standards) out into the range. They flew straight. They had the perfect trajectory. They satisfied my exploratory-assertive motivational system in a profound way. Had I been able to move to Florida and afford a couple of weekly lessons from him, he might have been able to teach me to hit them that way consistently.

Such mastery, to Toski, was an integral part of the pleasure of golf. We played a round the following day so I could get a sense of what a playing lesson from an expert was like (again, all in the interests of literature). For most of that day, I played as I generally do in the presence of excellent golfers, which is to say abysmally. I almost kneecapped Toski when I skulled a chip on the first hole. He was moved to tell a short joke that circulates among teaching pros:

"What do you think of my execution?" the pupil asks after a typically bad shot.

"I'm in favor of it," the pro replies.

On the sixteenth, Toski hit his usual crisp draw into the middle of the fairway, perhaps one-hundred-and-seventy yards from the hole. I for once managed something approximating the swing he'd tried to teach me the day before and was lying only ten or fifteen yards behind his ball. We waited for the group ahead of us to clear the green. I took advantage of the lull to ask him how it was that golf had managed to hold his attention for more than sixty years.

"It gives me peace of mind like nothing else," he said. "It's got beauty, sunshine, and fresh air, and it's challenging. I don't need a lot of people cheering. I just need to be out here figuring out how to play each shot."

The green cleared. I hit a five-wood that landed in the fringe, a bit short. Toski took a five-iron and played a shot that never rose more than ten feet into the air. It hit the turf ten yards in front of the green, skipped up the neck at the end of the fairway, and came to rest hole high, about ten feet from the flag. To me it looked as if the ball were quivering, it had been struck so smartly. It was a specialty shot, almost an extended bump-and-run, the kind of shot that a good player adds to his repertoire if he plays a lot in windy Florida conditions.

"That's almost a lost art, that shot," Toski said. "It's not taught anymore. Now it's all hit it high, bomb the green, and sink the putt. But I like the artistry of the game. There are so many shots you can play. It's like playing all the instruments in a fourteen-piece orchestra. If you recorded them all separately and then blended the recordings, people would say, 'That's great music. Who's in the orchestra?' And I would say, 'Bob Toski plays every instrument.' "

He smiled, perhaps just a little abashed at his own egoism yet unable to suppress his cockiness and his pride in his own mastery. I was so inspired that I almost birdied the next hole.

Toski signed my scorecard at the end of the round—a souvenir. Emboldened by a few good shots on the back side, I asked him whether there was any realistic hope for me to shed my slicer's hack and join the ranks of players with actual golf swings.

Toski tried to break it to me gently. "It depends on how much you're able to work on it," he said. "Do you live in a place where you can play year-round?"

No, I said. I didn't.

He shook his head sadly. "Gotta play year-round," he said.

He was like a kindly priest again, but this time he was telling me that I didn't have a true vocation and maybe I'd better start thinking of a life outside the seminary.

I thought of something he'd said at lunch the day before. Most people, in Toski's opinion, are destined to slice the ball. It's because of the way their motor skills develop as infants and children. They reach for things with their right hands. When they start to play games, they learn overhand motions with their right hands. When they come to golf, their instincts are all wrong. They reach out with their right hands, and they're bound to cut across the ball when they swing. (I know. That's what Johnny Miller means when he talks about coming over the top.)

Perhaps Toski was right about destiny and the golf swing. Or perhaps it was the damaging effects of the two or three months I take off each winter. Whatever the case, my swing has remained my swing. When I got home, I spent a season thinking about accelerating the move of my left shoulder, about starting the downswing with my right knee, about the feeling of hitting the drive off a ramp. Those thoughts gradually lost themselves in the welter of other thoughts flitting around my mind, the residue of other lessons. Once in a while I see a shot like the ones Toski had me hitting on the range that morning in Florida. Most of the time it's more of the same—pulls left and fades right. I try to manage them.

Putting and chipping, I reasoned, might be different. I couldn't recall any childhood indiscretions that ought to prevent me from rolling the ball straight along the ground. So on a reporting trip to southern California, I went to see Paul Runyan for a short-game lesson.

In the annals of the game, no player is as renowned for his skill around the greens as Runyan. The emblematic match and shot of his career occurred on the same day, in the summer of 1938, in the finals of the PGA Championship at the Shawnee-on-the-Delaware resort in Pennsylvania.

He was playing Sam Snead, a young Snead, who in his day was as long as Tiger Woods is in ours. Most of the gallery, like the golf press, expected Snead to thrash Runyan. After all, Snead could reach all the par fives on the golf course in two shots. Runyan could reach none of them.

Nevertheless, Runyan thrashed Snead, 8 and 7. He did it with his short game. Runyan let Snead go for the long holes in two shots. As often as not, Snead wound up near the greens but not on them. He was in the thick, deep rough growing in the course's rich, alluvial soil—most of the holes on the Shawnee course being on an island in the middle of the Delaware River. Runyan would lay up fifty or sixty yards short of the green, then pitch on and make the putt for his birdie. Snead had to hack the ball out of the rough toward the hole. He couldn't match Runyan's birdies.

The crushing blow in the match was delivered on a par three. Snead putted his ball between Runyan's ball and the hole. In those days the stymie rule was in effect. Runyan couldn't ask Snead to mark his ball and putt over the mark.

He had to get around Snead's ball. It looked as if he was bound to lose the hole.

Instead, he took a niblick and chipped over Snead's ball and into the cup.

By the time I scheduled a lesson with him, Runyan had been studying the short game for approximately three-quarters of a century. His study had begun in Hot Springs, Arkansas, where he was born on a farm in 1908. The road from the Runyan farm to the local school passed by the Hot Springs Country Club, and Paul Runyan began hanging out there. He'd play a couple of holes on the way to school. At recess he'd sneak onto the fifth hole and play it till the greenskeeper caught him and chased him. By the time he was fourteen, he had finished his formal education and become an apprentice to the pro at Hot Springs, James Norton.

Necessity caused Runyan to focus his attention on the short game. He was a wisp of a boy and not much bigger as a man. He realized early on that if he wanted to compete with bigger players, he would have to beat them around the greens. So he studied putting and chipping. He copied the putting style of a Hot Springs member who putted with both elbows bent, palms facing each other around the grip of the club.

Runyan continued to develop his techniques in his first job as a head pro, at a nine-hole club called Concordia in Little Rock. The course didn't get much business on weekdays, and Runyan passed the time putting and chipping on the greens—which weren't actually green. They were oiled sand. He found that balls pitched onto sand greens with any loft acted unpredictably when they landed. They might release toward the hole, or they might burrow down into the sand and stop. He got much better results with a chipping method that eliminated loft as much as possible, getting the ball onto the putting surface at a low angle and letting it roll. His chipping method resembled his putting method.

Both methods worked. Runyan led the Tour in money won a couple of times back in the '30s. He played on Ryder Cup teams. He won the PGA twice. He did this even though, in his prime, he weighed perhaps one hundred and twenty pounds and could drive the ball maybe two hundred and thirty yards.

When his tournament career ended, Runyan got teaching jobs at clubs on the West Coast and continued to ponder and experiment, seeking the best techniques for making a golf ball roll into a hole. In those years a lot of the club members he taught were scientists and engineers in the aerospace industry. They awakened in Runyan a nascent interest in mathematics.

Though his education had been limited to eight grades in Arkansas, Runyan had a keen aptitude for geometry and a fascination for the planes and angles of the game. Their precision appealed to him. He started asking his pupils questions. He had the president of Convair Air calculate how a change of a mere inch in the radius of the swing would affect the point at which the clubhead met the ground, all other factors being unchanged. (The answer was that it would make the clubhead strike the ground more than a foot behind the ball—an inspiring swing thought if ever there was one.) He started thinking of the putting stroke in terms of angles and levers.

He applied what he learned to the way he stroked his own putts. Gradually his style became more and more eccentric. In his sixties he decided that the reverse overlap grip he'd been using for fifty years was not as efficient as a grip with the hands split apart about an inch. He kept experimenting and in his seventies began putting with a grip that had the hands split so wide that the lower hand was down on the steel shaft of the putter. He found that it was very stable but that it was not too good at controlling distance on longer putts. So in his eighties he went back to the grip with the hands split about an inch apart. He would, he thought, hold the radically split grip in reserve in case he started getting yippy in his old age.

As he neared ninety, Runyan didn't act like old age would catch up with him soon. He was abstemious in his personal habits and religious about exercising. Bettering his age when he played golf was no longer a challenge. He still played a lot of rounds in the seventies. He entered an occasional super seniors event and did well enough so that the money he earned from tournaments in the 1990s was greater than the amount he'd earned when he led the Tour in the 1930s.

When I found out I was going to Los Angeles, I used the number Rotella had given me, called Runyan, and set up an appointment. He taught at Arroyo Seco, a municipal driving range a few miles from the Rose Bowl in Pasadena. It was a busy place, with a par three course, a practice green, and a couple of dozen stalls with green mats for hitting longer clubs. The practice green was strewn with branches that had fallen in a heavy storm the night before.

Runyan showed up precisely on time. He wore an old brown fedora and a flannel shirt. His golf bag was nearly as big as he was. We chatted for a few moments about his health and a few mutual acquaintances. The overwhelming impression was that this was a kind man, a man any child would be lucky to have as a grandfather.

He proceeded to impart a small portion of what he'd figured out about putting.

The problem with most people's putting, he said, was that too many levers got into the act.

Levers?

Levers were skeletal and muscular systems that moved the club, he explained. The hands and wrists could be levers. The shoulders could be levers. The entire body could act as a lever. What he'd found was that the more levers a golfer let into the act, the harder it was to coordinate them and the greater the likelihood that a lever would fire out of sequence, fire too strongly, or fire too weakly. The clubface at the moment of impact would not be moving squarely toward the target.

The best lever for moving the clubhead, he had found, was the shoulders. His method was designed to make sure that the shoulders, and only the shoulders, propelled the club.

"The ideal position for the hands in chipping and putting is for each palm to be facing inward and upward at a forty-five-degree angle," he explained. "An angle of about ninety degrees is formed between the arms. The shaft of the club, if you extended it upward, would split this ninety-degree angle. Thus, each forearm approaches the shaft at an angle of about forty-five degrees."

I scratched my head. I have a brother who teaches high school math. I thought about calling him. I had only the vaguest idea what Runyan was talking about.

"I'm not much good at geometry," I said.

"Well, this is simple stuff," he replied. "The geometry of the full swing is much more complicated. For instance, if you took an iron and gave it one degree less loft, how much lower to the ground would that make the ball two hundred yards out from the point of impact?"

I confessed that I had no idea.

"Well, you should!" he reproved me.

A trifle exasperated, he did what Toski had done, which was to physically place my hands and arms around the shaft of my putter so that all the planes and angles were correct. The position felt odd. If my putter shaft had a sharp blade mounted in the butt, I could have used Runyan's grip for *seppuku*. In fact, it seemed more suited to that.

When I took a few experimental practice strokes, I found that the position encouraged me to move the club with the shoulders. The hands and wrists were locked into opposing positions that canceled each other out. That was why Runyan had resorted to a split-hand grip. In the more traditional overlapping grips, one hand had a stronger position on the club and a chance to dominate the stroke. With the split hands and the forty-five-degree elbow angles, everything below the shoulders was more or less inert.

It was time to try actually putting a ball. Runyan lined one up on the grass below me, about four feet from a hole. Before I could hit it, he stopped me.

"You're not aimed right," he said.

I thought I had been aimed at the hole.

"A lot of people can't aim properly," he said sympathetically. He had consulted eye specialists, he told me, to learn about the triangulation involved in eyesight and how it affects a person's ability to read greens and line up putts. I nodded as if this made perfect sense to me. Runyan adjusted my putter a degree or so to the right.

I swung the blade. It scuffed the ground an inch behind the ball. The putt went about halfway to the hole and stopped.

"It might take me a while to get the hang of it," I muttered.

"That's all right," he said. "I'm in no hurry."

I knew he wasn't, but I was also aware of the fact that he was nearly ninety. How much time could he have to wait for me to get the hang of it?

I tried a few more putts. Something strange happened. The balls began to roll into the hole, first from three feet, then from four, then from five. I stepped back to ten feet and continued to make putts—not all of them, but perhaps two-thirds.

"That's it," Runyan said. Once in a while he stopped me to tweak some aspect of my setup, being certain that I played the ball off the big toe of my left foot, that I maintained the forty-five-degree angles of the hands and forearms, that I kept the rest of my body still when I moved the single lever of my upper body.

I stepped back to twenty feet and sank a couple. I started feeling giddy, thinking of the Nassaus I was going to win with a putting stroke that was deadly from twenty feet in.

Runyan had me step off the green to try his chipping method. It involved the same grip and the same stroke as the putting method. The club varied, depending on how much fringe and rough the golfer needed to carry and how long he wanted the ball to roll.

Runyan had been renowned for the accuracy of his chipping. In his precise way he calculated once that he required an average of 1.97 strokes to get up and down from the near environs of any green; in other words, he'd chip in more often than he'd take three strokes. But his chipping method didn't work for me the way the putting style had. I had trouble regulating distance. I had doubts that I would ever be able to find practice time to develop touch with all of the irons in the bag, which his method required me to use. And I had doubts that the style would work well for balls buried in the rough. I got a few chips close to the hole, but not any more than I would have chipping in my accustomed, more traditional style.

Before I was aware that the time had passed, my hour was up. I did not want to keep a man of Runyan's age any longer than he had agreed to come. So I paid him and shook his hand. I picked up his bag. He protested that he could carry it himself. But when I insisted, he allowed me to take it to his car. He drove off.

Tentatively, I went back to the practice green. I tried a few putts, half expecting that Runyan, like a leprechaun, had taken his magic with him.

They went in.

I felt a surge of confidence. I stepped back to fifteen feet, then twenty, then twenty-five. Balls kept rolling into the hole. It was as if I had developed a new telekinetic power. I had only to look at the hole and will the ball into it. The ball obeyed. It was a form of what Bob Rotella called "playing with the eyes." See it and do it.

It was an odd feeling, stepping up to a long putt and believing, almost knowing that the ball was going in the hole. I reminded myself that this was just a shaggy practice green at a driving range in Pasadena, that there were no subtle breaks in these putts, that I knew exactly where to aim. I still couldn't diminish the feeling that my body had become a precisely tuned machine for rolling golf balls straight.

The next day the feeling was largely gone. I tried as best I could to duplicate the grip, the posture, the feelings that Runyan had taught me. I could almost hear his raspy, aging, and gently encouraging voice in my ear as I putted at a course up the coast from Los Angeles. But something had changed. I was no longer a ball-holing machine. I was my old self, albeit with a new grip and a new stroke. When I three-putted the third green, reality had reasserted itself.

I did not give up. I still use Runyan's grip and posture when I putt. I try to recapture the confidence I felt as balls started to go in during that lesson. I think my putting has in fact improved a bit from what it was before I met Runyan. But as time has passed, the memories of that day in Pasadena have started to fade around the edges. So has the sense that I can expect to hole putts from twenty feet. When one of them goes in, I am afraid, it is as often the result of a fortuitous combination of a bad read and a bad stroke as it is the result of design.

The putting stroke, in that sense, is like the full swing. A golfer can be so close to the right mechanics, so close to grace and fluidity, power and accuracy, that they seem to be separated from him by nothing more than a transparent membrane. But that's as close as most of us are going to get.

I can only imagine what golf must be like for those who spend their time on the other side of that membrane. Like Runyan and Toski, they can find in the mechanics of striking the ball an endless vein of curiosity, exploration, analysis, tinkering, and refinement, much as those who understand physics and mathematics can enjoy thinking about a unified theory of space and time that makes no sense to the rest of us.

I am left with a feeling about the mechanics of the game that is not unlike something I once heard from a pit boss at a casino in Atlantic City. I had asked him where the poker tables were, and he explained that the casino maintained only a small poker room on the top floor.

Why? I asked.

It was not, he explained, the operation's bread and butter. Slot machines and games where the house's income was greater, like blackjack and roulette, occupied nearly all the prime floor space. Poker was a courtesy to those guests who liked it. "It's there for youse," he said, "if youse want it."

That's where I would rank golf's mechanics in a catalog of the pleasures of the game. If you are the sort of person who wants to delve into the complexity of the swing, who finds it fascinating, who can master it, fine. I respect you. I envy you. It's there for youse if youse want it.

Plato and Tiger Woods

Why is it, let us ask ourselves, that mankind consents to hold prowess in sport in such high esteem?

—Haultain

At about the time Tiger Woods won the 1997 Masters by twelve strokes, breaking the old tournament scoring record, I was reading Plato. To be honest, I was reading a fragment of Plato in *Great Books* by David Denby, an account of a writer's return to college to audit the basic courses in humanities and Western civilization and see how the modern campus was treating the canon. Apart from its central purpose, the book could also serve as a quick refresher course for adults like me who have forgotten, or never quite learned, their Aristotle and their Montaigne and who are occasionally perplexed when they read an offhand reference to something like "Kantian ethics."

The text at issue was one I did vaguely remember from college, Plato's analogy of the cave. Plato asks his students to imagine humanity as a group of prisoners shackled from birth to the walls of a cave. Their bonds pin their heads so they can see only what is directly in front of them—the opposite wall of the cave. The cave has an entrance and there is a fire going in it, casting light into the interior. Between the prisoners and the fire someone erects a screen, and behind the screen they bring objects—statues of people, animals, things. The objects cast shadows on the wall of the cave in front of the prisoners. The prisoners, of course, take the shadows as reality. If their captors project the shadow of a rose on the wall and call it a rose, then the prisoners think the shadow *is* a rose.

Occasionally, though, a prisoner gets loose. He makes his way out of the cave and sees the world in its true splendor. He sees roses and understands the difference between a real rose and the shadow that his fellows have seen on the wall of the cave. The idea, of course, is that human knowledge and achievement are in a primitive state, and what we think we know is really just the vague shadow of the truth. In Plato's ideal state the rulers would be enlightened philosophers— those who had, in effect, gotten out of the cave. They would be required to return to the cave and tell the prisoners what they had seen. They would bear witness to the ideal, to the forms that most of humanity has seen only as shadows. They would be both philosophers and kings.

I had no desire to be ruled by a philosopher-king, but it struck me that Plato was on to something about Tiger Woods and the fascination of golf. There are some fortunate spheres of human endeavor where we sense the existence of an ideal far superior to the reality we are familiar with. The artist may have brilliant images tumbling about in his mind like clothes in a dryer. When he tries to catch them and set them down on canvas, he realizes that what he paints is only a clumsy approximation of the sleek and beautiful ideas he was trying to express. They are the best he can do. But the beautiful images remain in his mind, enticing him to paint again. A physicist may sense the existence of a perfect, unified theory that explains all natural phenomena. The best he can hope to accomplish with his life's work is to uncover one small detail.

Golf, in its way, is one of those endeavors with a distant yet perceptible ideal, and this, I think, has an enormous amount to do with its appeal. Anyone who plays gets a vague sense of the ideal game, the game as it could be. It's a game of consummate power, astonishing grace, and gratifying precision. In this ideal form of golf, par would be something like 54 because the players would never miss a green and they would never need more than one putt. Maybe par would be 36 because no one would need to putt.

Most of us, of course, never come close to achieving this game. Our own efforts resemble not the rose but the shadow of the rose on the wall of the cave. We know the ideal exists, though, because we get occasional flashes, sightings. We step onto a tee, look down at the fairway below, and somehow know that we are going to drive the ball long and straight, maybe with a controlled little draw at the end, into the middle of the fairway. Then we do it. Or we squat behind a forty-foot birdie putt and suddenly see the line that will take the ball into the hole. We hit the putt and it follows that line, winding sinuously toward its goal. It falls in.

Golfers revere the players who seem to come closest to fully realizing this ideal game. That is why, I think, tournament golf has always been a sport in search of heroes. The greatest eras in golf have been those in which players like Jones, Hogan, Palmer, and Nicklaus were at their best. The least attractive eras have been interregnum periods like the decade or so after Nicklaus and Tom Watson passed their peaks. Those were years in which the golf press grumbled about players without charisma, about clones from college golf programs who played well enough to make a good living but not well enough to be great. We don't want plodders to win our major golf championships.

There are some team sports in which it is true that Americans love an underdog. Football is one. Nearly everyone likes to see Kansas State finally stick it to Nebraska. If the Pittsburgh Pirates played the New York Yankees in the World Series, it would be hard to imagine many people, outside the immediate households of George Steinbrenner and Rudy Giuliani, rooting for the Yanks. Americans identify with the little guy in those sports.

In golf, though, we want heroes to win. No one whose name isn't Casper roots for Billy Casper to beat Arnold Palmer in the 1966 U.S. Open. No one wants Gene Homans to upset Bob Jones in the final of the U.S. Amateur in 1930. We want to see Palmer and Jones win. No one thinks, "Well, Jones has already won three majors this summer. It's time for someone else to take a turn." We want to see him win the Grand Slam.

This is because golf fans, in contrast to most football fans, generally play the sport they watch. They have a rooting interest in the fortunes of the player who seems to be leading the exploration of the possible at any given moment. He is showing them the way. They don't want him to falter. They want him to break through to still greater feats. If he must be beaten, they want him to be beaten by a player even more heroic.

That explains why, in the spring of 1997, Tiger Woods was such a phenomenon. Scarcely a magazine could be published without Tiger on the cover. Corporations vied for his endorsement. Books about him were commissioned. Books about his upbringing were commissioned. Some of this, no doubt, was due to the person Tiger was. For society at large, he seemed to embody a new and updated version of the American ideal—young, lithe, talented, and handsome, with the added cachet of being multiracial. He promised to be a Frank Merriwell for the new millennium, an athlete who embodied the possibility that America might yet put her racial divisions behind her. For golfers, though, Tiger's popularity had much more to do with the way he played golf. This was a man who played No. 15 at Augusta with a driver and an eight-iron. This was a man who, to revert to Plato's analogy, had broken free of the cave and seen the roses close up. This was a man who expanded the scope of a golfer's dreams, who showed us a little more clearly what we were striving toward.

The more I thought about this, the more I wanted to ask Tiger about it. I wondered if he saw himself as I saw him. I knew he'd been at Stanford for three years before he turned professional. I assumed there was at least a chance he'd read Plato. Did he think of himself as the man who got out of the cave, as our champion, our explorer of the ideal?

I had occasional opportunities to ask him. Once in a while a magazine would assign me to write something that required interviews with players on the PGA Tour. The easiest way to get the interviews was to show up at a tournament site on Tuesday and Wednesday, the days before the competition began, cadge a temporary press credential from the director of media relations, look for the player on the practice tee, and buttonhole him.

That, of course, applied only to players less celebrated than Tiger. Tiger was in such demand that had he allowed himself to be buttonholed on the practice tee by everyone who wanted to ask him a question, he would never have been able to practice. Instead, whenever Tiger entered a tournament, he held a press conference on Tuesday.

These press conferences occurred in the tournament media centers, which were in enormous air-conditioned tents or in a basement storage area that the host club generally used for carts or mowers. In the front of the room there was always a large scoreboard and a stage. Long rows of tables—workspace for reporters—filled the center of the room. On the periphery were communications tentacles, the fax machines and phone banks, as well as the all-important supply of soft drinks. The press conference room was generally partitioned off from this work area.

The press conferences were not exactly forums for intimate and extended conversation, but I had only one question for Tiger. So I started going to his press conferences whenever I was at a tournament. They were always jammed. They were always impressive. He showed up in his golf clothes, his Nike hat pushed back off his face. He looked relaxed. He handled himself far better than some presidential candidates I'd covered.

The questions generally fell into three categories. Writers from cities further down the line on the Tour wanted to know if Tiger was going to play in their towns. ("Tiger, does Milwaukee hold a special place in your heart?") Writers from the big golf publications wanted a quote from Tiger about an upcoming major. ("Tiger, do you enjoy links golf?") And the local writers were looking for an angle for a Tiger feature. ("Tell me why you enjoy being around Michael Jordan, Tiger.")

Tiger smiled often, parried the questions he didn't want to answer, and usually gave the writers what they needed. (Milwaukee did hold a special place in his heart, but he couldn't fit it into his schedule this year. He liked links golf because it allowed him to be more imaginative. And Michael Jordan was a great guy whom he regarded as a big brother.) He was a polished performer.

Only occasionally did a casual observer get a chance to sense the weight of the load he was carrying, the burden of all the lawyers and agents and hangers-on who had found remunerative employment with Tiger, Inc. Standing by the practice tee at the Mercedes Championships one morning, I watched as a marshal, an elderly white-haired volunteer, asked Tiger to sign a copy of a biography that had been published by a writer named John Strege. "I can't sign that. It's unauthorized," Tiger said briskly, and walked past. I felt a stab of sympathy for a kid who, at the age of twenty-two, had become part of an operation whose rules and mores required him on occasion to be rude to elderly men.

Meanwhile, I hesitated to ask my question about Plato. In

the environs of the Tour's media centers, it seemed somehow inappropriate, like asking the the president some oddball question about his saxophone when everyone else wanted to ask about his position on tax cuts in the next budget cycle. But finally, one Tuesday at La Costa, after a couple of writers had exhausted the subject of the trajectory of Tiger's new irons, there was a pause. I raised my hand and the Tour's media moderator recognized me.

"Uh, Tiger," I said, "I was wondering if you ever read Plato and the analogy of the caves and, if you did, whether you see the golf game you play as analogous to breaking out of the cave and seeing things in their ideal form?"

The Tour media moderator's mouth dropped open. I heard a perplexed, perhaps angry muttering sound from a couple of writers in the row behind me.

Tiger looked at me, deadpan.

"No," he said.

Then he flashed the big smile that had graced a thousand magazine covers. He passed his right hand through the air over his Nike hat.

"Whoosh," he said. "Right over my head."

The Game as It Might Be

The phantom of perfect success flits ever before the ardent golfer.

—Haultain

Tiger's answer notwithstanding, I thought that there was an ideal golf that Plato would have agreed fit the concept he was trying to convey. Tiger had gotten closer to this ideal in the last sixty-three holes of the 1997 Masters than perhaps anyone ever had. But golf dangles the ideal before all of its devotees, giving them glimpses of the game as it might be. Once in a while someone actually catches this chimera and plays his ideal game for an extended period, accomplishing something remarkable. And this renews the faith of the rest of us, keeps us coming back to golf. We believe that next season, the next round, the next swing we might somehow elevate ourselves to this pinnacle of grace.

Jack Fleck, I thought, might know how this could happen. Fleck had one week of surpassing brilliance as a golfer, when he won the 1955 U.S. Open at the Olympic Club in San Francisco, defeating Ben Hogan in a playoff. He had never played so well before that week. He never played that well afterward. But for one week, he had it. When *The Majors of Golf* magazine asked me to write a preview story before the 1998 Open at Olympic, I suggested a look back at Fleck's transcendent week. The magazine agreed.

I wrote to Fleck in care of the PGA Tour. A couple of weeks later I got a letter from him, postmarked Magazine, Arkansas. He owned and ran a course there called L'il Bit o' Heaven, he wrote. He included a phone number. I called. "It's interesting that you got in touch," he said. His voice sounded hale and forceful. "I've been thinking about publishing something, an autobiography maybe, that would reveal what happened at that tournament."

Ah, I thought. That sounded like a secret. I made a date with him for the next week.

To get to Magazine, I took a morning flight to St. Louis, then transferred to a small plane bound for Fayetteville, in the foothills of the Ozarks. There I rented a car and drove a couple of hours down U.S. 71. It was poor country, full of mobile homes and rusting old cars mounted on blocks. Magazine, population 793, was in the rearview mirror almost as soon as I entered it. I was looking for the landmark Fleck had given me, a yellow sign mounted on a tree outside town with the single word "Golf" on it. I turned, and the pavement gave way to dirt. The road wound through a few farms wedged into the little valleys between hills. It was early December, and the land was brown and ragged. A couple of miles on, I saw what looked like a broad pasture dotted with flags instead of cows. This was L'il Bit o' Heaven.

I pulled into an empty parking lot and knocked on the door of the tiny white clubhouse. The 1955 U.S. Open champion emerged. He was broad-shouldered and erect, with a face dominated by bushy salt-and-pepper eyebrows. He wore greenish plaid pants and a blue sweater. His grip, when he shook hands, was firm.

"Welcome to my golf course," he said.

He was clearly proud of it, so I asked him how it had

come to be. Fleck said he got the idea a couple of decades ago when he was working as a club pro in southern California and someone approached him about building a small course for President Nixon next to Nixon's home in San Clemente. Fleck doodled a sketch of a course that required half the land a regular course did, with nine greens. It had two holes on each green, with two sets of tees. The Nixon project fell through after Watergate, but Fleck didn't forget the idea. Twenty years later he bought some land in Arkansas and built it.

Fleck obviously had not had an enormous budget. The greens had some drainage built underneath them and a finer grade of grass than the coarse turf surrounding them. The tees were raised a couple of feet and covered with rough Bermuda grass. It was very basic golf. The green fee for nine holes was six dollars. When I tried to pay it, Fleck waved me off. I was his guest. My clubs had gotten lost somewhere between St. Louis and Fayetteville. He lent me a set.

The first hole at L'il Bit o' Heaven was a short par five, about four hundred and fifty yards. Fleck pointed out the green to me. Had he not, I would not have known which of the four or five greens visible from the tee to aim at. He pulled his driver from his bag and teed a ball. He reached out with the club and tapped the ball with the sole of the clubhead, knocking it a fraction of an inch closer to the ground without dislodging it from the tee. It was a pro's move, I thought, the sort of mannerism only good players can have. He set and swung. He had a long, slow, graceful motion with a lot of leg drive. He hit a draw that wound up thirty yards past my tee shot, in the left half of what served as a fairway. Not bad, I thought, for a seventy-six-year-old.

We got into a golf cart and set off. I complimented him for designing a course that opened with a short par five, the easiest sort of hole for the average player to par.

"Most modern designers have no regard for the people who pay the freight—the public and the members," he said. I got the sense he identified with the people who pay the freight more than, say, Jack Nicklaus does when he designs a course.

We hit woods up close to the green and got our pars. Fleck drove on to the second tee, which backed up to a woods and had a jagged rear edge. "Had some beaver problems," he said. "They built a dam back there and the creek flooded and took half the tee."

How, I asked, had he solved the beaver problem?

"They went away after my son, Craig, found the right kind of shotgun," Fleck said.

No. 2 at L'il Bit o' Heaven is a par three, maybe one hundred and forty yards. Fleck took an eight-iron and gouged an enormous divot with his swing. To say he hit it fat would be an insult to fat people. The ball rose weakly into the air and plopped down about fifty yards in front of the tee.

"Hit the big ball that time," Fleck said, which is exactly what my brother Bert says when he lays sod over a ball during his semiannual round of golf at the beach each summer. (The big ball being Earth.)

It was hard to imagine Hogan, even at seventy-six, hitting a ball that way. It was still harder to imagine Hogan ever saying, "Hit the big ball that time" and smiling about it, as Fleck had done. But Fleck could swing that way and say that. He was obviously quite mortal. And yet Fleck had beaten Hogan, the immortal.

A couple of holes later, a cold drizzle started. "Why don't we go in?" Fleck suggested. "You've seen most of the course."

That was fine with me. I wanted to find out whatever secret he had to reveal about ideal golf—the golf he'd played to win the U.S. Open.

We walked through the little pro shop to an adjoining restaurant—a double-wide trailer with the interior walls removed. Pictures of Fleck at Olympic forty-three years earlier hung on the wall by the window. I was struck by how closely his clothing then resembled Hogan's—the same drab colors, devoid of advertisers' logos, the same white cap. We sat down on plastic chairs at a long table with a checked cloth. I asked him how he got started in golf and if it was true that Hogan had been his hero.

"I got started in golf because I wanted to make money," Fleck said.

He was born in Iowa. The Depression began for the Flecks a few years sooner than it did for the rest of the nation. When Fleck was five years old, in 1926, his father lost the family farm at a foreclosure auction. The Flecks moved into a house in the small town of Bettendorf and lived largely on the vegetables they could grow on a two-and-a-half-acre lot. They never starved, but money was scarce. Fleck remembered a winter afternoon when he was about ten. His school closed because it was so cold that the furnace couldn't heat the classrooms. Each child was given a dime for bus fare home. Fleck hitchhiked home in the freezing cold rather than spend the windfall.

The Western Open was played in Davenport, Iowa, in the summer of 1936, when Fleck was fourteen. It was Fleck's entree to the game. He got work as a forecaddie at the tournament and stayed on afterward as a caddie, making forty-five cents a round. After he'd been caddying for a while, he acquired a five-iron and started to play. He could remember sleeping in a bunker on warm summer nights so he could rise at dawn and play before the course opened. In his first competition, a caddies' tournament, he shot 89, using clubs borrowed from a member. He was self-taught.

Nevertheless, Fleck started to think about a career in golf. He was not, by his own account, very studious. Even if he had been, there was no money for college. Fleck was looking at a career spent scrapping for scarce jobs in factories and foundries that manufactured farm equipment. Golf seemed like an attractive alternative.

At about that time Fleck heard of Hogan. He followed the

Tour results in the newspapers and kept a notebook in which he jotted down the leading players, their scores, and the money they earned. Toward the end of the Thirties, Hogan's name started to appear in it.

Fleck got up and poured himself a cup of coffee. He offered me a Coke.

He recalled that he got on a bus the first time he tried to play professional golf. It was the winter of 1939. He rode as far south as Poplar Bluff, Missouri, where he noticed that there was no longer any snow on the ground. To save money, he got out of the bus, cashed in the rest of his ticket, and thumbed his way to San Antonio, where he entered the Texas Open.

Fleck had little luck as a tournament player. He won almost nothing and he scraped together a living working summers as an assistant pro in Iowa, entering tournaments on the pro circuit each winter. He spent four years in the navy during World War II, and it was not one of those stints in which he taught admirals to draw the ball. He never touched a club. The first round he played after his discharge, he shot 93.

Fleck was stubborn. He did not give up. He got a job as the pro at a municipal course in Davenport called Duck Creek. He kept trying to play tournament golf each winter, using the money he'd earn each summer selling balls, renting carts, and giving the occasional lesson.

He often studied Hogan during those winter tournaments, but surreptitiously. During practice rounds most of the pros played with their friends, betting and having a good time. Hogan usually played alone, pacing off yardages, trying different clubs for the shots he anticipated, preparing himself for the tournament. Fleck used to walk behind him, out of sight, standing behind trees, watching what he did.

But Fleck's game reminded no one of Hogan's. He did not have Hogan's icy demeanor. Instead, he had a temper problem. Not infrequently he would enter a tournament, shoot a

78, and withdraw angry. Once, in Phoenix, he three-putted the last two holes of the opening round and got so mad he jumped in the car and drove straight back to Iowa, even though his score for that round was 69.

That was the other big weakness in Fleck's game—putting. He had a flawed stroke, he recalled. He cut across the ball. He used to ask touring pros like Dutch Harrison for putting tips, offering ten percent of whatever he might earn to the man who could cure him of three-putting. No one could.

"I was the worst putter you ever saw," Fleck said. I doubted that. I thought I saw the worst putter every time I played golf. But I didn't argue with him.

In the summer of 1955, Fleck entered the U.S. Open and qualified at Lincolnshire Country Club in Illinois. He went to San Francisco with career earnings of about $7,500. Few contestants were less heralded.

Hogan, on the other hand, was indisputably the best player in the world. In 1953 he had perhaps the best season any professional golfer has ever had, winning the Masters, the U.S. Open, and the British Open. He was renowned for the precision of his ball striking and his tenacity under pressure. He also had a club company, and just before the Open his company had outfitted Jack Fleck. Hogan personally delivered the final two clubs, a set of wedges, to Fleck as the Open began.

The results of that Open are encrusted in legend and myth. The Olympic Club that year had grown perhaps the deepest, most punishing rough of any course in Open history. It was well over ankle high just steps off every fairway. The field average that week was 78 strokes per round. Hogan shot 287, seven strokes over par, and seemed to have won. He handed the last ball he used to Joe Dey of the USGA and said, "This is for Golf House," the USGA's museum. In those days, however, the leaders did not necessarily play in the last group of the day. Fleck was still on the course, and he came to the final hole needing a birdie to tie. He got it. The next day, in a playoff that seemed to call for more energy than Hogan had left to give, Fleck shot 69 and won by three strokes.

The myths about that Open, Fleck said with some bitterness, seemed to him to have been spread with the intention of making his victory seem more flukish than it was. One published story said that Fleck bogied the first six holes in the first round and was about walk off the course when Walker Inman, his playing partner, calmed him down and persuaded him to finish. I checked the record. Fleck was only one over after six holes.

Some of Hogan's friends circulate a tale about the par three third hole in the playoff round. In their version Fleck hits his tee shot into a bunker. Hogan hits his nearly stiff. Fleck skulls his explosion and barely stays on the green. He's upset, embarrassed, and still away. As he walks to his ball, he says, "Sorry to be holding you up, Mr. Hogan."

To which Hogan, rather than responding with an icy stare, responds with soothing kindness, "Don't worry, Jack. Take your time." Fleck calms down and sinks his long putt. Hogan misses his short one, and momentum in the match shifts. The implication is that if Hogan hadn't gone out of his way to be nice to Fleck, Fleck would have fallen apart and the playoff would have ended differently.

Again, a good story. But again, it didn't happen. "I never said a word to Hogan, and he didn't say anything to me," Fleck recalled. And he had a newspaper clipping, a stroke-by-stroke account of the round, that shows that he hit the fringe of the green on No. 3 with his tee shot, putted up, and made a relatively routine par.

Fleck said he'd gotten used to hearing that his win was a fluke, but he'd never liked it. "I never got many compliments on my golf that week," he said. "But I did play good golf."

Granted. But why, I asked, did he happen to play the best golf of his life at the U.S. Open? How could he vault from being less than mediocre, by professional standards, to being good enough to defeat the best ball striker who ever lived? And why was he never able to play that well again? What was the secret he'd hinted at?

Fleck got a little vague.

"Maybe it was self-hypnosis," he said. "There were two or three California psychiatrists who said I hypnotized myself."

Did he believe that? Did he hypnotize himself?

"I just had self-composure, that's all," Fleck said. "I'd been working on it for years."

He didn't know why he suddenly mastered the trick of composing himself on a golf course that was set up to be maddeningly difficult. He did remember thinking that he liked the course. "There was no out-of-bounds, no creeks, no lakes, no penalties. Just golf," he said. "I knew that driving would be important and I was a tremendous driver."

But his putting. How had he managed to putt so well?

Fleck replied that he'd putted poorly in his first round, when he'd shot 76. Then, on the fifth hole of the second round, an odd thing happened. "I just had a great feeling in my hands," he said. He started putting well. He did not have a three-putt for the rest of the tournament.

That feeling in the hands, I thought. That was it. That was a symptom of the elusive, beatified state that golf dangles in front of us—ideal golf. Could he describe it further?

"What it is, I don't know," Fleck said. "I don't know to this day." Then he repeated himself. "I just had a good feeling in my hands."

He could remember feeling blessed during the playing of the tournament. He told me that when he came to the eighteenth hole of the fourth round needing a birdie to tie Hogan, he did not feel anxious or nervous. He recalled looking at the scene in front of him—the closely mowed fairway, the green, the trees, the hayfield rough, the enormous crowd in the natural grass amphitheater encircling the green—and thinking, "If this isn't heaven, what is?"

That feeling stayed with him through that U.S. Open and

never returned. Fleck played for a few more years on the Tour but never duplicated what he'd achieved at Olympic in that week.

And the truth was, he didn't know exactly why.

But Fleck was adamant about one thing. His experience with ideal golf might not have been completely under his control, but it was not a matter of pure luck, either. He resented the stories suggesting that only luck, and dumb luck at that, could have enabled him to beat Hogan. He felt he had beckoned the golf he played that week, helped it to happen, by working for years to improve his putting and control his temper.

I'd encountered another U.S. Open champion whose story also suggested that ideal golf was most likely to settle upon someone who'd worked hard to achieve it. A magazine assigned me to write a story prior to the 1997 Open at Congressional about Ken Venturi, the man who'd won the previous Open at that course, back in 1964.

I called Venturi at his home in Florida, and he invited me to come down and see him. He lives on the Gulf Coast in a community where the radio station plays recordings by singers like Keely Smith and Jack Jones, songs from "back when music was music." It's a neighborhood of large, slow-moving Cadillacs and a McDonald's where the regulars come in and stay all morning, taking advantage of the free coffee refills. Venturi answered the door in gray slacks and a green wind shirt. He led me to an office, not bothering to point out the small trophy case that contained, among other things, his Open medal.

I had, of course, watched and listened to Venturi for years on the CBS golf telecasts. I knew the general outlines of his career and of his triumph at the Open. What I hadn't known were the details of how far Venturi had fallen in the years prior to that Open and how hard he'd worked to climb back. Sitting behind a desk, he told me.

As a boy in San Francisco, Ken Venturi had stuttered. That was the first thing he thought to say when I asked him about how he got involved in golf. It was the dominant fact of his childhood. Teachers told his mother he would never speak properly.

I was surprised. I had never heard him stutter on television. "On television I'm all right," Venturi said. "Face-to-face I'm all right. But if you'd tried to do this interview by phone, you'd have heard it." Stuttering was something he had overcome but never cured. He still considered himself a stutterer. When he did fund-raisers and speeches for children who stuttered, he told them, "You think no one on television can possibly understand how you feel. Well, I can."

Ashamed of his handicap, he had taken refuge in a sport he could play alone, without having to talk to anyone—golf. Somehow the hours he spent in solitary practice, learning the rhythm of the golf swing, talking to himself all the while, had helped him to learn the rhythms of the spoken word, to bring his voice under control. He had gone to college, held down a job selling automobiles, courted and married a pretty girl, and spent two years in the army on the front lines of the Cold War.

And he had become one of the best young golfers of his generation. He won the California State Amateur and attracted the attention of Eddie Lowery, a San Francisco auto dealer whose roots in golf went as far back as Francis Ouimet's watershed triumph for America at the 1913 U.S. Open. Lowery, then ten, was Ouimet's caddie when he beat Harry Vardon and Ted Ray. Lowery knew everyone in golf, and he arranged for Venturi to get some polishing from Byron Nelson.

Nelson, in his gentle way, took apart Venturi's game and reconstructed it. When they finished, Venturi had an iron game reminiscent of his tutor's. He was not an overly long hitter, but he had a graceful, powerful motion through the hitting area. His approach shots flew crisply and accurately.

Still an amateur, he was invited to the 1956 Masters. He led the tournament after three rounds, but on Sunday he stumbled to a humiliating 80 and lost by a stroke. The wound from that day never quite healed. Forty years later, commenting on the 1996 Masters for CBS, he would be unable to bring himself to use the word *choke* in describing Greg Norman's fourth-round collapse and loss to Nick Faldo. He identified too closely with what Norman was going through.

Venturi picked himself up and went on. He turned pro and joined the Tour in June 1957. He won twice in that abbreviated rookie year, four times in 1958, twice in 1959, and twice in 1960.

In 1961 a car he was riding in was broadsided. Nothing was broken, but muscles were torn in his back and neck. Venturi should have taken time off, but he couldn't afford to. He kept playing, flattening his swing in an effort to ease the pain in his neck. He lost his grace, his rhythm. And he started to slide, making virtually no money in 1962 and 1963.

He found it hard to handle playing poorly. He started to drink, to the point of getting in altercations in bars. He was disagreeable. The club where he was the touring pro let him go. His clothing company let him go. He and his wife separated. Golf tournaments that once had welcomed him forgot his name.

He touched something close to bottom in September of 1963. Venturi walked into a bar called Tropics on Geary Street in San Francisco and began drinking Jack Daniel's. The bartender was a man named Dave Marselli, an ex-football player from the University of San Francisco. He had known Venturi in better days, and he did not like looking at the Venturi before him.

"Ken, what are you doing?" Marselli said. "You've got everything going for you. But you're ruining yourself." Marselli paused. "I believe in you."

"I appreciate that, Dave," the golfer said. "Give me a drink."

"You sure?" Marselli asked.

"Give me a drink," Venturi repeated.

Marselli poured another whiskey. Venturi drank it. Then he took the empty glass, leaned over the bar, and dropped it in a trash can.

"Dave, I give you my word," he said. "I will not have another drink until I win again." And he walked out of the bar.

It was the kind of melodramatic pledge an experienced bartender has probably heard a hundred times, and Marselli can be forgiven if he discounted it. But Venturi had at least a slight basis for making it. His injuries had finally started to heal. When he dropped his glass in Dave Marselli's trash can, he had a realistic chance to practice for the first time in several years.

So he began. For three weeks he hit only nine-irons. It was the only club he could swing properly. He got out the notes he had made from the lessons with Nelson and gradually repaired his swing. His practice sessions at the California Golf Club were such that he would return to the clubhouse at dusk and fall asleep, exhausted, in the locker room.

When he returned to the Tour in 1964, he was no longer a star. He didn't have a Masters invitation. He had to beg for sponsors' exemptions to other tournaments. Finally, toward the end of spring, he could feel his game start to come together. He entered the Open and got through the local qualifier in Memphis. He begged an invitation to the Thunderbird Open outside New York and headed east.

A lot of friends stuck by Venturi during this time of troubles, and one of them was Toots Shor, the New York saloon keeper and restaurateur, who had a soft spot for athletes down on their luck. When he heard Venturi was in the area, Shor sent a car for him. Venturi dined well at Shor's that night, still not drinking. And when he tried to pay, his waiter told him his money was no good.

Shor walked Venturi to the car. "Toots," Venturi said, "I am going to make it. And I promise you I'll be back."

"I know you will, pal," Shor growled. "And when you're ready, I'll be waiting for you."

Venturi's game picked up. He placed third at the Thunderbird and sixth the next week in Detroit. In the sectional qualifying for the Open, he shot a 77 in the first round but persevered. He closed with a 70 and made the field.

When he got to Washington, though, one more humiliation awaited him. President Johnson hosted a lawn party at the White House for past Open champions and current Tour stars on the Tuesday evening before the tournament started. Venturi was not invited.

Summer in Washington can be oppressive. There are times when a high pressure system takes up residence just off the coast and seems to squat there, fending off any cooling winds. The air grows hot and still, then humid, then dirty, until walking outside can feel like taking a steam bath in a dumpster. The 1964 Open was contested at such a time. Temperatures rose into the high nineties, perhaps higher in some of the sunlit and breezeless hollows on the Congressional course. The heat baked out the rough, turning it brown and thin. It hardened the greens. Local players know that golf in such conditions is partly a game of fluid management: keeping sweat out of the eyes and off the grips, drinking a lot of water to replace what the body is losing.

Venturi tried to conserve his strength. He played only nine holes on Tuesday and nine on Wednesday. His game was still not what it once had been. He did not, for example, use a tee when he hit his driver. He was afraid that would prompt him to pull up as he came through the ball, a habit he had developed when he was favoring his neck. So on driving holes, he kicked up a little turf with his shoe and placed the ball atop it, forcing him to stay down on his shots. He would play the whole tournament that way, hitting low sliders off the tee. But he felt his biggest shortcoming was still the strength of his mind.

"You regain your skills faster physically than you do mentally," he told me, thinking back on it. "And the mental game is the line between great and really great."

Venturi began the tournament a long way from either. On the front side Thursday, he fluffed two sand shots and left them in the bunker, going out in 38. He steadied himself on the back nine, however, and finished with a 72. On Friday he was steadier still, and he shot 70. It gradually became apparent that Congressional's long par fours, which called for accurate long-iron approach shots, suited Venturi and his iron game more than they did some other players. But he was still barely in contention. Tommy Jacobs, who shot a brilliant 64 on Friday, had the midway lead at 136. Arnold Palmer, with a 68 and a 69, was a shot back.

As Venturi left the locker room Friday, he was given a letter that had arrived from a California priest, Father Francis Murray, who was counseling him. Father Murray's letter mixed spiritual exhortation with practical advice. "You are truly the new Ken Venturi, born out of suffering and turmoil, but now wise and mature and battle-toughened," he wrote. Father Murray told Venturi that his victory would inspire people everywhere who were struggling with adversity. He told him to take it one shot at a time on Saturday and get his birdies early—it was going to be hot.

That evening Venturi left his motel room and drove to a church. He knocked on the door of the rectory and asked the priest to open the sanctuary for him. The priest obliged, and Venturi knelt in the darkened nave and asked God to help him believe in himself.

Father Murray, it turned out, was right about a lot of things, beginning with the weather. By midmorning Saturday, Congressional was beginning to roast. Venturi did exactly as he had been advised. He started getting his birdies on the first hole, where his ten-foot putt hung on the lip for what seemed like eternity—and dropped.

It was a good omen. He went on to birdie the fourth, fifth, and sixth. At No. 9, Congressional's longest hole, he hit a precise one-iron to the proper lay-up point, fired a wedge at the pin, and rolled in a delicate eight-foot birdie putt. Jacobs and Palmer, meanwhile, had gotten off to shaky starts. Palmer missed the first five greens and three-putted the sixth on his way to a third round 75. Jacobs bogeyed the eighth and ninth to drop to three under. As he made the turn in the third round, Venturi was leading the Open.

He continued to play well, with another birdie at the thirteenth. But at No. 17, looking at a twelve-foot birdie putt to go seven under, Venturi started to lose it. He stopped sweating; his body had no more fluid to give. He began to shake.

He had not, he recalled, taken any precautions against the heat. Coming from northern California, he was unaccustomed to the conditions of a Washington summer. "I didn't drink anything during the morning round," he said. "Maybe one glass of water. I didn't think anything about it. I was just sitting on go, and when I got out in 30 strokes, the game was more important. I'm not thinking, 'Should I get a drink?' I'm humming along."

Now he was no longer humming. He was dizzy. He bogeyed the final two morning holes, allowing Jacobs to pass him again. He had shot 66, and he was two strokes behind. But that was not his immediate concern. His immediate concern was survival. Until 1965 the Open concluded with thirty-six holes on Saturday. Venturi still had a round to play.

There was a station wagon to take players around to the locker room, and Jay Hebert rode with Venturi. "He told me later that I didn't even realize he was next to me. I was lying with my head back on the seat rest. My eyes were rolled back in my head. He thought I was dying." Venturi lay down on the floor of the locker room, sipping water. Someone summoned Dr. John Everett, a Congressional member who was chairman of the Open's medical committee.

"He was trembling, very pale, and sweating profusely," Dr. Everett told me from his retirement home in Florida. "I thought he was suffering from heat exhaustion. I told him I didn't think he should go out for the final round. I told him it could possibly be fatal if he tried. He told me, 'I've come this far and I've never been here. I'm going to try.'"

Venturi had no recollection of this conversation. He did not remember how he got from the locker room to the first tee that afternoon. About the only thing he remembered from the intermission in the locker room was stepping onto the scale. He weighed one hundred and sixty-six pounds. When he started the morning round, his weight had been one hundred and seventy-four.

Dr. Everett armed himself with ice, towels, water salt tablets, and iced tea. He advised the golfer to put on an undershirt to absorb sweat. Venturi did; he also got a new glove. Then the doctor suggested that Venturi avoid walking in the high grass because it would take more energy. Venturi took that advice to heart.

They went back out into the sun. Looking back, Venturi figured that his condition was almost a blessing. It was all he could do to focus on the shot immediately at hand. He had no energy to spare for thinking about his opponents, his position in the tournament, or anything else. He was so intent on his own game that when the round was over, he would hand his playing partner, Ray Floyd, a blank scorecard. He had not written down any of Floyd's scores. He still, he told me, could not remember a single shot Floyd hit. It was as if he were playing in a tunnel.

"It was reflex, instinct," he recalls. "I don't know why I cut one shot or drew another. I just did it. I was so sick that I didn't feel the pressure. I knew where the next tee was and I went there. And when I looked at the pin, it looked like a telephone pole. I took aim at it. That's where I was going."

This, I thought, was the same state of grace that Jack Fleck had gotten himself into, the state with which golf teases all players. In Venturi's case it was brought on by several factors. First was all the preparation he had done all those years. Venturi's path to his ideal golf had started in boyhood when he had taken up golf as a refuge from stuttering. It had taken him through heartbreak at the Masters, through lessons with Byron Nelson, and finally to those exhausting rehabilitative practice sessions at the California Golf Club late in 1963 and early in 1964. Finally, the withering heat at Congressional had shorn him of the ability to think about anything but the shot at hand. He was, in a sense, unable to come apart the way he had at the Masters back in 1956. Coming apart would have required him to think of all the extraneous, distracting factors that a psychologist like Bob Rotella counsels players to avoid. Venturi didn't have the energy to think about them. It was all he could do to handle the basics—hit the ball, survive the heat.

In this inspired daze Venturi, splay-footed and pale, slowly made his way over the burning hills and valleys of Congressional, with Dr. Everett administering a steady stream of salt tablets, cold towels, and iced tea. Palmer and Jacobs fell away, but Venturi was barely aware of it. Joe Dey, who was following Venturi, at one point asked him if he wanted to look at the leader board.

"I said no," Venturi recalled. "I had no control over that. And I didn't want to change that zone I was in."

When he got to the eighteenth tee and hit his drive down the fairway, he saw an old friend from San Francisco, Bill Hoellie, in the gallery.

"I bent over to him and said, 'How do we stand?' " Venturi recounted.

"Just stay on your feet and it's yours," Hoellie told him.

Slowly, very slowly, Venturi did that. He got to his ball and hit a four-iron, blocking it to the safe side, the right side, but into a bunker. As he made his way down the hill, he could hear the roars of the gallery. He could see the scoreboard beyond the pond behind the last green. His was the only name followed by red figures, so he knew he had a little cushion.

Then he hit a shot that, months later, when he saw it on film, made him break out in a cold sweat. He took a big swing and exploded the ball out of the bunker. "It was the dumbest move I ever made," Venturi said. "I could have chipped it out and been totally safe. Trying to blast it, I could have skulled it into the pond and let Jacobs back into it."

But the shot worked, stopping twelve feet from the hole. As he looked over the putt, he thought it would bend slightly right. He stroked it—a push. But at the last instant the ball inexplicably curled left and went in. Venturi dropped his putter and raised his arms like a referee signaling a touchdown—not in triumph, as most assumed, but in shock. "It can't break left," he recalled of that putt. "But it was just the way it was supposed to be, I guess."

He made his way to the scorer's tent, gave Floyd his blank card, and then sat there, paralyzed with fear. He had to sign his scorecard, but he could not be certain that all the numbers were correct. He thought of Jackie Pung, his fellow San Franciscan, who had lost the Women's Open for signing an incorrect scorecard. Try as he might, Venturi could not get his frazzled brain around the numbers on the card in front of him.

Finally, he felt a hand on his shoulder. It was Dey.

"Go ahead and sign it, Ken. It's correct," Dey said.

Venturi signed and became the U.S. Open champion. He never won another Open, though he won twice more that summer. Within a year he developed circulatory problems in his hands. He had surgery and played for a few more years, but he could not recapture the state of grace, the brilliance he had that weekend at Congressional. By 1966 he was trying his hand at television commentating, and a few years later he retired to go to work for CBS.

But that was all in the distant future. The immediate future was a phone call from the White House switchboard, which tracked him down in his motel room on Sunday morning. The president of the United States, he was told, was requesting the pleasure of his company for lunch.

"With no disrespect to the president of the United States," Venturi said, "tell him thank you very much, but tell him I'm dining with Toots Shor."

He made his way to New York. Cab drivers honked and waved to him as he walked down 52nd Street. He opened the door to the restaurant and saw Shor sitting at his usual table with Joe E. Lewis and Frank Sinatra. All three men jumped to their feet and started to applaud. So did everyone else in the place. It was, Shor told him, the only standing ovation in the history of the restaurant.

Venturi sat down with his friends and ordered a glass of wine. In accordance with his pledge to Dave Marselli, it was the first drink to pass his lips since that night in the bar on Geary Street. It tasted, he recalled, rather good.

Fleck had a feeling in his hands. Venturi worked his way into an inspired daze. They were different players, with different games. Certainly Venturi had a more distinguished career than Fleck's. But there was at least one thing they had in common, apart from their single Open championships. In describing their peak performances to me, neither one used the phrase "I played over my head."

In fact, both of them suggested that they felt that the rounds the world considered extraordinary were, in a sense, quite normal. It was all the other rounds, before and after, that were abnormal. Fleck felt that the 1955 Open was the one time when the world saw Jack Fleck's real game, freed for a week of his problems with putting and temper. Venturi felt that the 1964 Open represented his true game, without the debilitating effects of his nerves and his injuries.

This, I think, is the essence of golf's allure. Playing well seems so attainable, so normal. Surely we'll start doing it on the next shot. It will be like that forever after.

My own brief encounter with ideal golf shares at least that aspect with Fleck's and Venturi's. It was, oddly enough, connected to Venturi. Five months after I interviewed Venturi, on a sunny morning in early June, a friend called and said that a mutual friend was inviting us to play a round that afternoon at Burning Tree.

Burning Tree is a quiet club in the Washington suburbs that for many years was the unofficial home course of the White House. Presidents from Eisenhower to Bush played there. When Eisenhower was president, the Secret Service had a direct line to the pro shop. Kennedy used to pop into the kitchen to check on the soup of the day. It might still be the course of presidents except that it was founded by a couple of men from the Chevy Chase Club who got tired one day of waiting behind a group of women. Burning Tree began and remains for men only. As such, it has fallen from public favor with Washington's political elite, or at least that part of the elite that runs for office. It has perhaps gained compensating favor from those who enjoy golf on a classic course with the added piquancy of being politically incorrect.

I like women golfers, but since I was not contemplating a run for the presidency, I managed to stifle my ethical qualms about playing a round at Burning Tree. I drove out there. A guard at the front gate checked my name off on a list of guests. I drove past precisely edged beds full of precisely planted rows of impatiens. I saw a practice tee equipped with piles of snowy Titleists. It was a lovely, warm, late spring day with the mugginess of summer still over the horizon.

In the parking lot I bumped into Venturi. He was in town

for the telecast of the Kemper Open and was about to play a round with some friends. We chatted for a moment. I asked after his wife, who was ill. As it happened, his group teed off directly ahead of mine.

I don't know whether Venturi's presence had anything to do with it, but I played the best round of my life that afternoon. And it was, in its way, as he and Fleck had described their ideal rounds at the U.S. Open. It felt not supernatural but strangely natural. I did not suddenly start hitting two-hundred-and-fifty-yard draws off the tee. I didn't knock any irons stiff. I didn't sink any long putts. I didn't feel the presence of spirits. I simply didn't make any serious mistakes. My drives all got off the tee and stayed in play. I never hit a ball in the water. When I missed a green, I chipped reasonably close. I got up and down a few times. I made nearly all the three- and four-foot putts.

This was, for me, ideal golf. There was a sense of calm control, of confidence. It was serene. It felt like I was finally playing the golf I should have been playing for years.

It was not until the final hole, when I chipped in for birdie, that I did anything extraordinary. "It's not polite for a guest to win all the skins," my caddie whispered to me as we waited for the others to finish. We giggled.

We adjourned to the locker room. At Burning Tree the banners of the government agencies that have been headed by members hang from the locker room ceiling, giving the place a sense of history and power, as well as the smell of sweaty hats. I changed my shoes. Venturi came down the aisle between lockers. I introduced him to my friends.

"Nice day, wasn't it?" Venturi said.

"Gorgeous," I agreed.

"Have a nice round?" he asked.

"Oh, seventy-five," I said, as if I posted that number a few times a month.

Venturi smiled, nodded. "Not bad," he said, and walked into the bar.

From that moment forward, golf has owed me nothing.

• • •

I have found that many golfers harbor memories of rounds like this. Some of them even publish their stories on Internet pages devoted to golf. I read one account of a "transcendent" round posted by a player named Richard White of Mechanicsburg, Virginia. I sent him a message and we agreed to play.

Richard turned out to be a pleasant man who looked like a pirate, with a shaven head and an earring in his left ear. He had a wrestler's body, with wide, sloping shoulders and short, powerful legs. He was from Texas originally, he told me, and he'd played a little golf as a boy. He worked as a computer programmer for a consulting company.

Richard had brought along a couple of friends, Dr. George Oliff, a radiologist from Richmond, and his son Bryen. Bryen worked with Richard, and it was Bryen who'd reintroduced Richard to the game a few years ago.

We were playing a tough course, a Mike Strantz design called Royal New Kent. A few months later it would become one of the few new courses, and few public courses, to be ranked by *Golf Digest* among the top 100 in the country. Strantz had supposedly recreated the feel of an Irish links course at Royal New Kent. That was dubious, fifty miles from the ocean. But he had, by dint of either natural terrain or massive earthmoving, indeed created some holes that wound among towering, grassy hills, protected by bunkers so deep that the only way to play from some of them was backward. It was a course that required a player to hit the ball crisply and straight.

Unfortunately, Richard began the day doing neither. He lost three balls on the first hole. I felt that this was my fault. I'd put him in the same spot I'd been in the first time I played with Rotella, the spot I'd seen many amateurs in when they played with the stars at pro-am events. Richard had written of a transcendent round, and a stranger had gotten in touch and arranged a game. Naturally, he wanted to do well, to show he'd not been exaggerating He wanted it too much.

After a while I was at least giving him reason to believe he wasn't the only hacker on the course that day. I dumped one ball in a swamp, then buried another under the lip of a fairway bunker. I had to drop from the unplayable lie. Richard and I were both wobbling a little as we walked onto the eighth green.

"This round reminds me of the Apache way of killing someone," Richard said. "They give the guy a lot of little cuts with a sharp rock, tie him to a tree, and let him bleed to death slowly. I can't get anything going. It's not my day."

I was pleased when he started to relax after the turn. He played the back nine in 43 strokes, chipping in on the seventeenth and parring the last to win two presses. We took our nine-dollar winnings and stood the Oliffs to some beers.

I asked Richard to tell me about the round he considered transcendent.

"It was a late afternoon in August a couple of years ago," Richard recounted. "I decided I had just enough time to play fifteen or sixteen holes before dark. So I went over to a course called Glenwood in Richmond. It's one of the old, old public courses. It's not in a great neighborhood. There've been some incidents there. Kids steal your balls and sell them back to you. An armed robbery. Guy got shot. Some people've started calling it Gunwood. But it was easy for me to get over there real quick and play."

Richard had been practicing that summer, whittling his handicap down to about ten. But he hadn't reached his goal of breaking 80, and given the daylight available, he didn't think there was any chance of doing it that day. He'd been paired with a man and his wife whom he didn't know. For whatever reason he relaxed. On the third hole he had about one hundred and eighty-five yards into the green, and he hit a five-wood to within three feet. He missed the birdie putt but realized that he was hitting the ball well. After nine holes the man and his wife went in. Richard kept playing. He caught up with another single and they started to play the last few holes. Twilight was deepening into darkness. Richard kept hitting the ball well.

He was, he recalled, quite aware of the score. In fact, he kept adding up his total and calculating what he would have to do on the remaining holes if he were to somehow finish the round and break 80.

But in another way he felt quite detached. "It felt like something took over beyond my own abilities," he said. "I had a difficult par putt on the fifteenth, a four-footer. The ball went right in the middle of the cup, but I had the sense of not being conscious of making the stroke or of putting. I was there. I knew I did it. But it was almost like watching myself do it."

"My best round was like an out-of-body experience," Bryen chimed in. "Like I was looking at someone else making the shots."

"Sort of a peace," George observed. Bryen and Richard nodded.

"I don't know how you get into that," George said. "I wish I could do it more."

"The sixteenth and seventeenth holes," Richard resumed, "I felt like I was hitting the shots but couldn't feel it. The shots were just sort of something that happened. I felt really detached. I wasn't even thinking anymore that if I shot par and bogey on the last two holes I'd have a 79. I was just going to the ball, totally blank. It was getting really dark. I thought, 'I've got to finish this.' On seventeen, a long par four, I hit my approach right of the green. I was thirty or so yards from the hole, behind a bunker. I just wanted to get it close for a par putt. But I had that blank feeling, and I popped it up over the trap and watched it trickle and run and disappear into the hole. It didn't seem unnatural, didn't seem amazing. It flowed out of this experience."

The fellow Richard had joined quit at this point, saying it was too dark to see his hand in front of his face. But Richard decided to finish. He knew he needed only a six to break 80. More than that, he was reveling in the way he felt. On previous occasions when he'd had a good round going, he'd gotten to the final few holes and tried to force results. He'd foundered. On this particular evening he felt that he could just let the results happen. It was a mix of confidence and detachment.

He could vaguely make out the final hole in the last bit of light, silhouetted by some headlights in the parking lot or lamps on the clubhouse porch. Fortunately for him, it was a short par four and he was familiar with it. He hit his drive and felt solid contact. He couldn't see the ball's flight, but he walked to the point in the fairway where a solid drive would land, and there it was. He pitched onto the green and made two routine putts for his par and a score of 77.

He went home. He felt like his body was humming, energized and exhilarated by what had happened. It was a feeling he could compare only to a sense he sometimes got when he was playing the guitar and composing music and notes seemed to flow from his fingers. "It was a buzz, it was spiritual," he recalled.

Richard was so taken by the feeling that he telephoned an older brother to tell him what had happened. The brother listened to the story and suggested that Richard had experienced a peak, a visit to the acme of his potential.

Richard occasionally broke 80 after that round, but he never quite recaptured that sense of detached confidence, of skill and control, of exhilaration. One of the reasons he played golf, though, was the belief that he would again experience it.

"It's like saying what God is," he said. "It's hard to describe. Maybe it was like I was in a trance. Like those whirling dervishes. They're doing something physical, they're doing that dance movement. But you can tell that they're somewhere else. You're aware and you're conscious, but it's almost like an outside force is making it happen."

"If we could bottle it," George sighed, "we'd have it made."

I went home and told my wife about Richard White's round and the sensation he'd described.

"It sounds like a flow experience," she said.

"What's that?" I asked.

"*Flow* is a book by a psychologist named Mihaly Czikszentmihalyi," she said. "You ought to read it."

I did. It soon became apparent that Dr. Czikszentmihalyi, who is on the faculty at the University of Chicago, had never played golf. But he wrote as if he were describing the feelings of people who did.

Czikszentmihalyi, citing Aristotle, believed that men and women are motivated, more than anything else, to seek happiness. Most of us, though, are a little confused about the source of happiness. We envision it as a static, passive thing. We will be happy when we are sitting in our dream house, next to our dream lover, surrounded by our dream possessions.

To the contrary, Czikszentmihalyi thought. Happiness is something we feel in the middle of the active, successful pursuit of something we want.

"We have all experienced times when, instead of being buffeted by anonymous forces, we do feel in control of our actions, masters of our own fate. On the rare occasions that it happens, we feel a sense of exhilaration, a deep sense of enjoyment that is long cherished and becomes a landmark in memory of what life should be like. . . . The best moments usually occur when a person's body or mind are stretched to their limits in a voluntary effort to accomplish something worthwhile," he wrote. He called these moments optimal experiences, or flow experiences.

For a swimmer, Czikszentmihalyi suggested, this kind of optimal experience could come from besting his personal record for a given distance. For a violinist it might come from mastering an intricate passage in a Mozart concerto. For a painter it might come when the colors on a canvas begin to form something new, something alive.

He described some of the common characteristics of these optimal experiences. They involve competence, creativity, and an element of difficulty. People do not have optimal experiences flipping hamburgers at McDonald's, no matter how competent they are at it, because no creativity is involved. Nor do they have them filling in the spaces in a paint-by-number picture. That is too easy. And the bar keeps getting higher. A young violinist might have an optimal experience mastering a simple folk tune. As his skills improve, playing the folk tune does not work anymore. He must master more difficult pieces to get the satisfaction the folk tune once gave him.

Optimal experiences generally involve a task of some kind, which gives people a clear goal and a sense of completion when done. They require intense concentration. "When all of a person's relevant skills are needed to cope with the challenges of a situation, that person's attention is completely absorbed by the activity. There is no excess psychic energy left over to process any information but what the activity offers. All the attention is focused on the relevant stimuli," he wrote.

One important element, he found, is a stream of feedback to the person involved in the activity. The violinist hears the notes he plays, perhaps senses the enjoyment of the audience. The painter sees the paint go on the canvas. This gives them a sense of control, and that sense of control is inherently enjoyable.

At this stage, he wrote, people tend to lose their sense of self-consciousness. They waste no energy trying to keep themselves in order. They're aware only of the task and the pleasant sense of completing it. Their perception of time may be altered. They may look up and see a clock and realize that hours have passed without their awareness.

Czikszentmihalyi found that competition frequently prevents an individual from attaining an optimal experience. We are most likely to achieve flow if the competition is extrinsic to the activity, if it allows us to focus our attention primarily on the activity itself, not on defeating someone. It's not likely, for instance, that you will have an optimal experience playing basketball if your primary concern is winning. You might have one in a pickup game in which you can relax and just enjoy playing.

The quality of our lives, he suggested, is defined by how often we can have flow experiences.

It seemed to me that if Czikszentmihalyi had asked his graduate students to design experiments to induce test subjects to have a flow experience, one of them might have invented golf. Golf fits all the parameters he discovered. It engages the body and the mind, demanding intense concentration. It provides the player with tasks and goals—finishing a round, posting a good score. It certainly furnishes feedback. Every stroke is a gauge of how well a player is doing. And its competitive aspect can be modulated so that the player concentrates primarily on his own game. That, indeed, is the best way to compete at golf—not to react so much to what an opponent does, but to play the course as well as you can.

The theory of flow seems to account for what Richard White described, the sense of losing himself, of barely being involved in the transcendent round he played. Czikszentmihalyi would have said that playing golf, concentrating on each shot, had focused all his psychic energy and relieved him of the usual distractions that make us feel as if our minds are being pulled in several directions at once. He had subsumed himself in the flow experience, the game.

It might account as well for part of what had happened to Jack Fleck and Ken Venturi. Each of them had somehow managed to turn the U.S. Open into a kind of flow experience, shedding in the process the nerves and tempers and putting flaws that had burdened them in the past.

Whatever it is called—flow experience, hot streak, career round—it's an intoxicating feeling. It's one reason we keep coming back, full of hope, to the golf course. To the uninitiated, I suppose, this might make golfers seem like greyhounds at a racetrack, chasing after a rabbit they will never catch.

But the greyhounds, I've noticed, don't complain. Neither do golfers.

Why Ayatollahs Don't Love Golf

You can detect national character in games.

—Haultain

Among the Shiites of Iran, it is customary to seek an omen before embarking on a journey. The Iranian opens his Koran at random and reads the first verse his eye falls on. If, for instance, it is Sura II, Verse 271—"To be charitable in public is good, but to give alms to the poor in private is better"—he may quietly and without display stuff some extra *toman* in the poor box at the airport. If the book falls open to Sura V, Verse 51, and he reads, "Believers, take neither the Jews nor the Christians for your friends," he might cancel his trip to Chicago. Or worse.

Something like an omen led me to explore the status of golf in Iran. I was in the Library of Congress doing some preparatory research for a trip to the Caspian Sea for *National Geographic.* I wandered from the Reading Room into Alcove Six. My eye fell on a thick green volume called *The Encyclopedia of Golf,* published in Britain some two decades earlier. I opened it up and looked for an entry on Iran. Portentously enough, there was one:

*When Prime Minister Amir Abbas Hoveyda inaugurated
the new 18-hole grass course at the Imperial C.C. in Tehran in
October 1970, before an elite gallery of Iranian officials and
club members, he ushered Iran into the world of modern golf. . .*

*The new Imperial Course was developed under a British
resident professional, Jack Armitage, once assistant to Archie
Compston at Wentworth. The course was inaugurated with ten
holes in play. The remaining eight were opened in 1972.*

*The course is situated just below the Royal Tehran Hilton
Hotel, overlooking the city, with the Elburz Mountains for a
backdrop.*

It was not hard to find out what had happened to Prime
Minister Hoveyda. He was executed after the 1979 Islamic
revolution, presumably more for his association with the shah
than for his association with golf. But on the fate of the Imperial C.C., the library's sources were mute. I was, though,
booked at the Hotel Esteghlal in Tehran—née the Royal
Tehran Hilton. So I packed an old set of clubs. I thought that
maybe a look at golf in Tehran, if it still existed, could shed
more light on the question of why people played golf—or
didn't.

My seatmate on the flight in from Frankfurt suggested that
I had correctly interpreted the omen. He was a plump, pros-
perous, and friendly Iranian, and as we approached Tehran, we
poured ourselves a last round of wine. I asked if he knew anything about the old golf club.

He smiled. "It's still there," he said. "But it was nationalized
after the revolution. It's called the Enghelab Sport Complex
now. Enghelab means 'revolution.' Any cab driver can take
you there."

I have worked in several countries governed by the heirs of
violent revolution, most notably Russia. I am convinced that

the ultimate end of such upheavals is bureaucracy. After seeing thousands of his countrymen taken from their homes and shot, the normal human being looks for a way to protect himself. He finds it in bureaucratic procedure. He makes sure that if and when he hears the knock on his door after midnight, he will have paperwork to prove that he has lived his life strictly by the book—in triplicate. In postrevolutionary societies people become afraid to do almost anything without approval from higher up. Thus it was in Iran.

My assignment in the country was simple and innocent. I wanted to drive up along the Caspian coast to the villages where fishermen catch sturgeon, watch them fish, then watch the sturgeon roe being processed into caviar. I noted all of this in my visa application, and when my visa was granted, I assumed, naively, that the government had approved of my intentions.

In reality, I had cleared only the first hurdle, approval by the foreign ministry. Once in the country, when I tried to arrange a visit to the fishery, I was informed I would have to check in with the Ministry of Culture and Islamic Guidance to get its approval for my "program."

This required some time. My first few mornings in Tehran were spent largely in the company of three inscrutable women in the reception office of the ministry's press counselor. They wore wimples and veils, long sleeves and long skirts. Only their faces and hands were visible as they typed, answered telephones, and politely asked me to please wait until their boss was ready to receive me.

This gentleman, when he finally did receive me, was in no hurry to put his chop on my papers. We had a long conversation, from which it became clear that in the view of the Ministry of Culture and Islamic Guidance, all Western media were part of a conspiracy to besmirch the good name and reputation of the Islamic revolution and to sow hatred for Iran in the hearts of the people of America. I refrained from expressing my own opinion that the government of Iran seemed quite adept at besmirching the reputation of the Islamic revolution without help from the Western media and that, come to think of it, I didn't recall seeing many Western journalists in the crowd that had seized the U.S. Embassy back in 1979 and laid the foundation for the present American attitude toward his country. I simply noted that I had an apolitical program and would appreciate his help. He told me to come back the following morning. The following morning he told me to report to the Ministry of Fisheries the morning after that.

So I had my afternoons to fill. I did the sorts of things that journalists do when they're cooling their heels in a strange country. I walked around the city, poking my head into markets and mosques, talking to whoever would talk to me, looking for scraps of information that might somehow be useful if I were ever to manage to get up to the Caspian Sea. After a couple of days of this, I was ready for a break.

I grabbed my clubs (hidden under a sporty, Islamic-green Arnold Palmer traveling bag) and hailed a cab. "Enghelab," I told the driver, who, as it happened, spoke English. A couple of miles from the hotel, the driver turned into what looked like a fenced park. He drove past an armed guard, then past a large poster with a picture of a woman wearing the black cloak called the *chador*. It was a reminder, the driver said, that sporting activities do not excuse females from the obligation to dress in a way that covers everything but their faces. Since women are allowed on the course only on Monday and Tuesday mornings, when male golfers are barred, I would be unable to assess how these strictures affect their play.

There was no sign of Jack Armitage or his pro shop. But there was a sign for a "golf office," which we found in a corner of a building otherwise devoted to wrestling. I asked the driver to wait while I made inquiries.

Armitage, it appeared, had been succeeded by an Iranian with a luxurious stubbly beard, wearing a sweatsuit and shower clogs, sitting behind a desk and watching cartoons on television. Pictures of Ayatollah Khomeini and Ayatollah Khamenei hung on the wall above him; an old bag of clubs lying on the floor was all that suggested I had come to the right place. He spoke enough English to understand that I wanted to play and to nod his head that, yes, this was permitted.

The green fee was fifteen thousand *toman,* the equivalent of fifty dollars in a government bank or about thirty-five dollars if you bought your *toman* on the streets. After he took my money, he gave me a scorecard, opened it, and with a pen crossed out the fourth, thirteenth, fourteenth, fifteenth and sixteenth holes. "Finished," he said cryptically.

Another Iranian had joined me in the office. He was short and wiry, with a thick mane of graying hair and a bristly mustache. He had a pull cart and a set of half-a-dozen aging Wilson Pro Staff irons and a battered Wilson three-metal. He put on a baseball-style cap of faded blue with "Nakita" written across the front, tucked the cuffs of his pants into his socks, and laced up a pair of Adidas tennis sneakers.

I asked if he minded playing with me. His eyes widened and he stiffened slightly when he heard my accent. But he agreed. For reasons that will become obvious, I will call him Parviz. He was a road engineer on vacation, and he had been playing golf for two years.

"What is your handicap?" Parviz asked.

"Twelve," I replied. Before I could add the standard cant about a shaky twelve, jet lag, and not practicing lately, he beamed.

"Twelve is very good here," he said.

I didn't know whether Parviz meant twelve was considered a sign of skill or just an auspicious number—twelve, in Shiite theology, being the number of imams who have followed the Prophet. It didn't seem like the place to ask.

We walked through a parking lot and a copse of trees, past an open field. In the near distance the dry brown slopes of the Elburz Mountains hunkered over the course. They reminded me of the hills that surround Tucson in the Arizona desert. I could see a flattened place in the grass and a couple of old wooden blocks, bare and weatherbeaten. There was a concrete marker in the ground, but whatever words and numbers it once bore had long ago worn away. It was the first tee.

I was reminded of the first time I had seen the Forum in Rome; there was a sense of grandeur that once was. The old Imperial course lay below us, tumbling down a ridge, across a streambed, and along a valley floor that canted gently away from the mountains to the north. But the course seemed to be disappearing before my eyes. I could see a green, the ninth, that looked recently mown. But the bunkers had filled with grass and weeds. The fairways had lost their definition under the encroachment of the native brown grass and wiry scrub.

The card said the first was a four-hundred-and-five-yard par four, dogleg left. Parviz insisted that I hit first. He pointed to a building crane on the horizon; that was the line. Perhaps too conscious of the need to uphold the honor of all American twelve-handicappers, I swung and found that my unwanted tendency to slice off the first tee had survived the journey across eight time zones. Once, the ball might have come to rest in the rough, but I was eighteen years too late for that. It kicked into the desert scrub.

Parviz, perhaps too conscious in his turn of the obligation to uphold the honor of Persian golf, wound up, fell back onto his right foot, and hit the ball with the heel of his three-metal, across the ninth fairway and into a jail of evergreens.

I asked Parviz if there was a Farsi word for Mulligan, afraid even as I did so that I might be responsible for corrupting the purity of Iranian golf.

"Mulligan? No," he said.

He took off at a half jog after his ball. I walked off in search of mine, which I found nestled in the grip of a desert weed. Parviz caught up few seconds later, carrying his errant ball in his hand. He dropped it in a patch of fairway grass twenty feet to the left of mine.

"What is Mulligan?" he asked.

"Nothing you need to know," I said.

I hacked my ball toward the hole with a wedge. Parviz addressed his ball, then stopped.

"Which is best grip?" he asked. He showed me a baseball grip. "This?"—he changed to an interlocking—"or this?"

Considering where my drive had landed, I felt unqualified to give a lesson on the overlapping grip. So I told him that Jack Nicklaus used an interlocking grip just like his. He smiled and smothered a four-iron into the weeds on the left.

I reached the green with another wedge. Parviz chipped from the fringe and stopped the ball ten feet from the hole. My par putt started out toward the hole and then broke sharply away from the Elburz, stopping a full eight feet away.

Parviz had a Leo Diegel putting style, elbows straight out, but he understood how the Elburz affected his putts. He rolled his in. Mine stopped a couple of feet short. He picked it up.

"Given," he said.

I stopped worrying about corrupting Iranian golf.

The second tee was visible from the green, but I could not have located the second fairway without a helicopter. Bushes had grown ten feet high in the streambed in front of the tee, blocking the view.

"Over that bush," Parviz pointed.

I caught the ball, and it flew where he had pointed.

"Like Sana Snead," Parviz grinned. "Turn and burn."

It was worth all the *toman* to hear someone compare my swing to Sana Snead's.

"Sana Snead is a great teacher," Parviz said as we walked up the fairway, picking our way through patches of wiry, foot-high fescue that were reclaiming habitat from the more delicate grasses of the old Imperial fairways. "But as good as David Leadbetter?"

"Better player," I said.

"I have a book by Tom Watson," Parviz said. "Is he a great teacher?"

"I wouldn't let him change your putting stroke," I advised.

Parviz's tee shot had come to rest in a pile of rocks and pottery shards someone had dumped to the left of the fairway. He picked it up, walked back to the fairway, and deposited it in the shortest grass he could find.

"In this case we can take and put here, yes?"

I considered trying to explain the rule on unplayable lies, but it seemed inappropriate.

"Sure," I said.

Parviz's second came to a stop near my drive. He picked it up and started looking for a favorable clump of grass.

"Is all right to move ball in fairway?"

Now I was beginning to feel a responsibility for the integrity of the game, like David Fay discussing the rules on a U.S. Open telecast. But what was a reasonable interpretation of the rules at a course called Enghelab?

"One club length," I suggested.

Parviz looked pained, like a newly baptized native who learns from the missionary that orgies are no longer allowed. "One club only?"

"One club," I said sternly. He complied.

My own shot was ten paces inside the one-fifty stake. I hit my normal seven-iron. It fell fifteen yards short of the green.

"Is that one hundred and fifty yards or one hundred and fifty meters?" I asked Parviz.

"Meters," he said.

"But the scorecard is in yards."

"Yes," he said.

No. 3, a five-hundred-and-forty-seven-yard par five, took us down toward the section of the course that was, as the man in the golf office had said, "finished." Now I could see why. Major construction was underway. I could see a bulldozer and a pair of surveyors at work. It did not look like they were trying to remodel the golf course. It looked like they were trying to destroy it. That was what the man in the office had meant when he said, "Finished."

I pushed my second shot into rocky waste ground. I took an eight-iron and aimed for the only flag in sight. The shot fell short, into a freshly dug ditch, and disappeared. Parviz came up and joined my fruitless search.

"Why did you hit it there?" he asked. "That is seventh green," he said, pointing to the target I had aimed for. No. 3, it turned out, was half hidden behind a large fuel tank. Its flag had disappeared. I took an X for the hole.

On No. 6, I found out why the course had survived for as long as it had. The founders of the Imperial C.C. had installed a stout sprinkler system, and it had continued working long after they had departed, impervious to the political changes in Tehran, like a Voyager satellite sending data back to Earth years after the engineers who built it had retired. For some reason, the system had turned itself on. The sixth fairway was awash in geysers of water, slowly revolving. My tee shot landed next to one.

This was a situation the golfers at Enghelab were used to. "I will stop for you water," Parviz said. He jammed the shaft of an iron into the sprinkler mechanism, halting its rotation. I hit my approach and we went on our way, dodging water all the way to the green.

Parviz, though, was not having a good day. On one hole he pulled his tee shot left into the arid waste, caught the next shot thin, and saw it bounce off a pile of riprap left by the construction crew, almost back to his feet.

"Golf some days is good and some days is bad," he observed. "Why?"

I smiled. "When I figure it out, I'll tell you," I said.

As we walked up the ninth fairway, I asked him why he had taken up a sport that the regime in Iran seemed to disapprove of.

"I had a friend who played, and he said it was a good

game," Parviz replied. "At first the walking was important to me." Indeed, Enghelab was in one way better than the old Imperial C.C. Golf carts had disappeared along with the shah, the cart paths were slowly crumbling back to dust, and the golfers walked.

"But then," he said, "I got a little better, and I started to feel that the game was good for my entire—conflution?" He groped for the word in English.

"Constitution?" I suggested.

"Yes."

I chipped onto the ninth green, then watched yet another short putt break away from the mountains and miss the hole.

"Why don't the mullahs like golf?" I asked as we trudged uphill toward the tenth tee.

"Maybe because Americans play it," Parviz said, smiling.

The Imperial C.C.'s clubhouse bar had gone the way of all alcohol in Iran, but there were a few plastic chairs and tables set up in the shade of a pine grove behind the tenth tee, and a foursome of Parviz's friends were sitting there having drinks. They invited us to join them.

Two of them had mugs of a familiar-looking amber liquid, and I asked if it was beer.

"Islamic beer," a man I will call Abolhassan laughed. "No alcohol." It was a malt beverage that tasted like cheap beer gone flat. The locals cut it with lemon juice and ice.

Abolhassan had been a member of the Imperial Club in the old days. "Everyone who was consequential in Tehran belonged," he said. "But most of the people who used the golf course were foreign expatriates."

After the revolution the Japanese and Korean traders who stayed in Tehran had kept the course going. Iranians had stayed away, for the most part, until the past few years, when the zeal of the revolution had started to ease a bit.

I still wanted to know why an Islamic government should be opposed to golf. Not far from Enghelab I had seen a propaganda billboard depicting a martyred Iranian soldier in green fatigues and a red headband. He was in paradise, which the Koran depicts as a place of lush, green grass and cool, flowing waters.

Lush, green grass and cool, flowing waters could describe a golf hole, I said—maybe the thirteenth at Augusta. So why not embrace golf?

"The culture cannot accept it," one of the men at the table said. He gestured toward the course. "To a thousand Iranians this is *golf.* To sixty million Iranians it is hitting a ball into a hole with a stick." He meant, I guess, that golf was profoundly and inexplicably alien to all but a few westernized Iranians, the way that quantum mechanics is inexplicable to all but a handful of physics initiates.

Now, Abolhassan said, the course was under siege. In the years since the course was built, the city's fanciest neighborhoods had stretched out and surrounded it. "The land here is worth billions," he said. "The Revolutionary Guards look at it and say, 'Why can't we have it?' Two years ago they took three holes. This year two more holes went."

Why?

"You don't ask," Abolhassan replied. "They have guns."

It was getting late, time for Parviz and me to play what remained of the back side.

At No. 12, a par five, my second shot disappeared into a pile of construction rubble left strewn across the fairway.

"Free drop from ground confiscated by the Revolutionary Guards?" I asked Parviz.

"Of course," he said.

We holed out and trudged across the wreckage of the thirteenth through the sixteenth, stopping at the tee of the seventeenth. A barbed-wire fence cut off the back of the tee. Behind it a building was going up, and two Revolutionary Guards in fatigues lounged on a pile of steel beams, watching us.

We teed off. One of the guardsmen had a brief conversa-

tion with Parviz. When we were out of earshot, I asked Parviz
what had been said.

"He wanted to know whether you were Japanese or Korean," Parviz advised me.

The guardsmen, he explained, come from the remote villages of Iran, and they know of the world only what the mullahs tell them. The mullahs had told them that only Japanese
and Koreans played golf in Iran. Therefore, since I was obviously not Iranian, I must be one or the other. It was quite logical in its context.

The guardsmen, I suspected, would be extending their
fence. Iranian Islamic culture was rejecting golf as the human
body rejects a transplant from an incompatible donor. The Islamic powers that still governed Iran were allowing, if not encouraging, the extirpation of the game. I thought about why.

There were some obvious reasons. One was that in the climate and soil of Iran, golf courses were hard to establish and
expensive to maintain, much as they are in the arid states of
America. In a poor country they were a luxury. Another was
the general aversion to things Western in the aftermath of the
1979 revolution. Golf was among those things—like Hollywood movies, rock 'n' roll, and mini-skirts—associated with
the old regime, with the West, and therefore anathema. As
Parviz had noted, it was enough for some Iranians to know
that Americans played golf to know that the game was sa-
tanic.

But I didn't think that the Iranian antipathy toward golf
could be explained just by climate and the anti-Western fer-
vor of its revolution. Around the world Islamic countries in
general are among those least inclined to golf, even where
their soil and rainfall are adequate and their governments and
populations are friendly toward the West. There is the occasional sheikh in Dubai or king in Morocco who builds himself a golf course. But in Islamic countries golf is largely a
sport for expatriates and a small westernized elite.

It may be that, as Ayatollah Ruhollah Khomeini once said, "there is no fun in Islam." The Koran enjoins games of chance. This is generally interpreted to mean gambling, but the injunction has a wider impact. Sport in general seems less evident on the streets of Islamic cities than it does on the streets of Europe. There are fewer basketball hoops, fewer soccer goals. Sports are played, but participation seems thinner.

But the most powerful factor working against golf, I thought, was the underlying communality of Iranian culture under the Islamic revolution. The Iran of the ayatollahs evinced little or no concern for an individual's opinions, tastes, or wishes. If the ayatollahs decided that the Koran forbade alcohol, then the entire society must forgo alcohol, even at home (though there were Iranians who surreptitiously flouted this law). Women could not decide for themselves what constituted modest attire for the street. They all had to wear the *chador.* I didn't think that a culture that imposed the *chador* was a culture in which golf would flourish. As Parviz's friend had observed, Iranian culture could not accept the game.

That's because golf is the most individual of sports. A golfer does not need anyone else to play. He can be content by himself, meeting the challenges of the game in his own way, looking out for his own constitution, as Parviz had said.

That, I thought, was why the ayatollahs disliked golf, why their agents, the Revolutionary Guards, were steadily eliminating it from Iran.

That, of course, and the chance to make a lot of *toman* in the Tehran real estate market.

Two of Parviz's friends from the pine grove joined us midway up the seventeenth, and we were a foursome as we teed off on the eighteenth. The sun was going down, turning the Elburz range a pale mauve. As we walked up the fairway, the wailing sound of a muezzin's voice wafted over the course from an unseen minaret, calling the faithful to worship.

Do golfers, I asked, ever stop what they are doing to pray at the appointed times?

The three Iranians all laughed, and Parviz dropped back a step until he was close to my side. He lowered his voice to convey something confidential, something bordering on seditious, which is why I have not used his real name.

"Most golfers," he said, "don't pray."

My Home Course

Golf is primarily the game of the Scot.

—Haultain

Another omen.

Some months before going to Iran, I was reading *A History of Golf* by Robert Browning. The author was describing the earliest written records of the game, a good many of which happen to be Scottish church (or kirk) records:

> *The registers of the kirk sessions from 1580 onwards bear testimony of the popularity of the game in all parts of Scotland. There are records of golfers being charged with playing on Sunday, "tyme of fast and precheing," at St. Andrews, at Perth, at Leith, at Stirling, at Cullen and at Banff.*

At Cullen? Until reading this passage, I had not known that there was a town in Scotland whose name I shared, let alone that it contained one of the world's oldest golf courses. I got out a good atlas and looked it up. It lay on the shore of the Moray Firth, on the northeast Scottish coast, on the road between MacDuff and Cawdor. MacBeth, it seemed, might have known of it.

I am not Scottish. My family is Irish. But it seemed as if I were being invited to visit, to look in Cullen for a part of the answer to the question of why people play golf. And in particular, why did golf take root in Scotland? Why does golf flourish in some countries and cultures and not in others, like Iran?

I knew the conventional answer. It was given quite well by Alistair Cooke in an article for *The New York Times* some years ago:

> *Golf was just what the Scottish character had been searching for for centuries. Namely, a method of self-torture disguised as a game, which could entrap irreligious youths into principles of what was to become first known as Calvinism and then . . . golf. The main tenets of this faith are that life is grim and uncomfortable and that human vanity cannot prevail.*

Cooke is a golfer, but he is also an Englishman. It seemed at least possible to me that this stereotype of the dour, pleasure-hating Scottish Calvinist was as much an invention of the imperial English mind as the drunken Irishman, the stubborn Welshman, and the promiscuous Frog.

I knew as well that there were reasons for the rise of golf in Scotland that had nothing to do with the Scottish character. They ranged from the ready availability of links land, with its natural grasses and subtle terrain, to the invention of the gutta-percha ball in the middle of the nineteenth century, an invention that made the game more affordable and enjoyable than it had been with the old ball, a leather sack painstakingly stuffed with boiled feathers.

Nevertheless, I thought that Haultain had been on to something when he called golf the game of the Scot. So when I booked my return flight from Tehran, I booked it through London. In London I got a plane to Aberdeen. In

Aberdeen I rented a car and set out to find the course with my name on it. It was September, and the harvest was coming in. I drove on narrow, two-lane roads hemmed in by low stone walls. In the fields, rye and barley were rolled into neat, tight, cylindrical bundles, waiting for pickup. Sheep grazed on bright green hillsides. Thick, gray clouds lowered on the horizon, and the sun broke through only in pale, isolated shafts, like spotlights.

An hour out of Aberdeen, halfway to Loch Ness, a sign announced that I was entering Moray Whisky Country. Some of the world's great distilleries were located in the region, making Scotch from the barley in the fields and the clear, cold waters I could see in the occasional brook. The thought of foreigners heading to dinner on these narrow roads after a day spent touring the distilleries made me slow down.

As darkness gathered, another sign informed me I had reached the Royal Burgh of Cullen. It was a small town, nestled in a cleft of the headlands along the firth, comprising two parts. The old town, called the Sea Town, was once a fishermen's village, and the houses in it were small and packed tightly around the harbor on the east side of Cullen Bay. The newer town, which had the shops and the school and the churches, was built on higher ground overlooking the bay. Most of the houses in both parts of the town were of the traditional Scottish gray granite, solid and small, with white lace curtains in the windows and stone chimneys.

It was, I would learn, a remarkable town. With a population of barely more than a thousand people, it boasted not one but two castles. The older, Findlater Castle, was a stone ruin built into a cliffside on a promontory high above the sea to the east of town. From the farm that occupied the land above it, a visitor could look down on the castle and the narrow neck of land that connected it to the rest of Scotland, watching the gulls and terns as they soared and swooped around the empty sockets of its windows and imagining the endless warfare that had prompted the local laird to build in such an impregnable, uncomfortable place. The second castle, Cullen House, was a massive, sprawling product of the seventeenth century, full of gables and turrets. It sat on a knoll overlooking Cullen Bay. A rough *tapis vert* of green pasture gave the castle a sea view.

Adjoining the Sea Town, on the eastern edge of the bay, lay the Cullen links. They were intensely green, bounded by a curving stretch of rocky beach and a massive promontory that towered perhaps a hundred feet above the sea. Here and there the grass of the links gave way to spectacular red crags. They looked like fountains of rock erupting from the ground to heights of fifteen, thirty, perhaps sixty feet. I wondered how anyone had routed a golf course around them. But in the gloaming I could see red and white flags. There was a golf course out there.

I checked into a hotel along the main road near the central square of the upper town. It was called the Seafield Arms. Inside the door hung a photograph of the queen and Prince Philip, taken outside the hotel entrance some years ago. She looked younger and, to my subjective eye, happier than she has in recent years. They were posed with the earl of Seafield, whose property the hotel then was. The Seafield Arms, however, had new proprietors, an energetic young couple named Herbert and Alison Cox. It was a small, friendly place, with chintz covers on the parlor furniture and a calico cat lounging by the fire, the sort of inn where a visiting golfer who stayed on the links past the restaurant's closing time would find that the chef had left him sandwiches and a bowl of the local fish soup, Cullen Skink, lest he go hungry.

I asked at the hotel if there was anyone in town who could tell me about the local history. They recommended I check with Duncan Wood, a historian who ran an antiques store down the street. I walked down to Duncan's shop, but it was closed and locked. I asked next door at a toy shop. They didn't know where Duncan was, but they promised to let him know I was looking for him. Five minutes after I returned from my stroll to my room at the Seafield Arms, Duncan was calling for me from the lounge.

"When they said an American was looking for me," he explained, "I just assumed you'd be here." It was a small town.

Duncan was a lean, agreeable young man, dressed in jeans and a denim shirt. We shooed the cat off the sofa and ordered tea.

I had missed Cullen's moment of prominence in world affairs, he told me, missed it by a considerable time. Back in 961, the armies of the lands that we know as Scotland, Denmark, and Sweden had clashed near the Cullen links. Three kings had died there, including King Indulph of Scotland. Three of the crags that stand near the first tee on the links were called the Three Kings in commemoration of that day. The town had passed most of the ensuing centuries in pleasant obscurity, although the earl of Seafield had been one of the signers of the treaty that unified England and Scotland in 1707.

Fishing had sustained the town through most of its history, Duncan said. But the fishing industry declined and died in the first half of this century. Some of it was overfishing. Some of it was the vagaries of the market; there had been times when Cullen fishermen threw their catch off their boats into the harbor rather than accept the prices the fishmongers were offering. Nowadays, when a Cullen man went to sea to make a living, he was probably headed for an offshore oil platform, over the horizon in the North Sea.

Tourism had also suffered in recent decades, Duncan said. There had been a time when Cullen had a steady flow of summer visitors, many of them trade unionists from Glasgow who came on the train. The railroad had stopped running to Cullen. And cheap jet fares to the Costa del Sol had offered withering competition. Only recently had tourism started to bounce back, assisted by the new ease of travel between countries in the European Union.

The House of Seafield had been yet another institution in Cullen to see hard times, Duncan told me. Once the family had been among the wealthiest in Britain. But by the 1970s the estate was in financial difficulty. Property was sold off. Cullen House was sold to a developer who remodeled it into thirteen luxury condominiums, bought up by wealthy Germans, English—"and Yanks, if you'll forgive the expression," Duncan said. The Seafield family had kept the old factor's house, the erstwhile home of its estate managers, and lived in it when they came to Cullen. Duncan had heard that feuds and disputes had broken out among the new residents of the Cullen House condominiums. This news did not seem to displease him.

Among the properties the House of Seafield had disposed of, Duncan said, were the links, which were endowed to the Cullen Golf Club.

The links were land too close to the sea, too vulnerable to flooding to use for cropland. They had functioned as common land, a kind of park for the town. Fishermen laid their nets out to dry there. People walked their dogs. Football players held games on the flat stretches. Bowlers bowled. And golfers played there. At times during the nineteenth century, relations between the various groups of links users had not always been harmonious, but gradually these conflicts sorted themselves out. The football players and bowlers found other lawns to play on. The fishermen stopped using nets. In 1892 Old Tom Morris, the patriarch of the modern game of golf, had come up from St. Andrews to lay out nine formal holes on the lower portion of the links. Another nine holes were added in the 1920s, primarily on the upper portion. The links were now considered primarily a golf course, although hikers and dog walkers were free to use them and did.

It would be nice to report that the links and golf had sustained the spirit of Cullen through difficult times, much as

Hollywood tells us that baseball has sustained America. It would be nice, but it would probably be inaccurate. Golf in Cullen was not a universal pastime. The Cullen Golf Club had five hundred and fifty full members, some of whom came from neighboring towns. The game was the pleasure of a minority, albeit a substantial one.

I asked Duncan if he himself played golf. He laughed and shook his head. He did not.

Did Duncan have any ideas about the appeal of golf to the Scots?

He smiled. "I used to think golf was a pursuit of small minds and morons," he said. "But now it just baffles me."

Duncan did, though, put me on to a possible source on the mind and culture of the local Scot of the nineteenth century, when golf burgeoned. A novelist named George MacDonald had set two novels, *Malcolm* and *The Marquis of Lossie,* in Cullen, which he renamed Lossie for the purposes of his fiction. I found them in a library and read them.

MacDonald, it turned out, was born in Huntley, a farm town twenty miles south of Cullen, in 1824. As a boy he spent his summer holidays in Cullen. He had studied for the ministry, and his writings were deeply spiritual. To the degree that they are read today, it is mainly by people who appreciate his devout, austere faith.

But in his day he was a popular novelist. Both *Malcolm,* published in 1875, and *The Marquis of Lossie,* published two years later, are stirring reads, full of melodramatic plot twists. A son, the eponymous Malcolm, is born to the Marquis of Lossie in a mysterious room in Lossie House. But the marquis is absent and is deceived into thinking that both the boy and his mother are dead. He remarries and has a daughter. Malcolm, meanwhile, grows up poor among the fishermen. But he is a noble lad, honest, dutiful, and brave. Eventually, not without many trials and tribulations, he is finally recognized as the true heir of the House of Lossie and becomes a model Scottish laird, kind to his people and reverent to his God.

If Malcolm played golf, MacDonald chose not to mention it. But the author gave his heroic Scotsman character traits that intrigued me. For one thing, Malcolm is a religious icon-oclast. He belongs not to the Church of Scotland (which is closely related to the American Presbyterian churches), but to a breakaway sect that emphasizes the supremacy of the individual's relationship with God. He refuses to allow any-one to dictate his beliefs. "It's my conscience I'm bound to follow and not your lordship's or any man's," Malcolm says defiantly.

For another, Malcolm hates being idle. He is industrious, almost obsessively so. He looks for things to do, ways to chal-lenge himself. One of the principles that guide his behavior is, in MacDonald's words, "The desireableness of a life is to be measured by the amount of interest and not the amount of ease in it." That brought to mind what Tom Doak had told me about the task of the golf course architect—to make each hole as interesting as possible.

It seemed to me that the traits MacDonald had depicted might be the real source of the affinity between golf and the Scots. A strong streak of individualism might account for the attraction of a game in which the player is essentially alone. A love of challenges and a respect for adversity help resolve the seeming contradiction of a game that is full of misfortune and difficulties, yet addictive.

I thought it might be useful to explore this hypothesis with some of the heirs of Calvinism. Through Duncan Wood I contacted the local minister of the Church of Scotland. He was not a golfer, but he said that a couple of the neighboring ministers were keen on the game. He put me in touch with David Ferguson, clerk of the presbytery ("clark o' the prez-bih-tree") for the Cullen district and minister in the neigh-boring town of Fochabers.

"Yes, yes," the Rev. Mr. Ferguson said when I broached my errand and invited him to play a round on the links at Cullen. He had a kind, soft voice with a gentle burr. He offered to recruit a couple of his fellow churchmen to make up a four-some. We set the date for a Thursday at half past noon.

The Cullen Golf Club occupies a one-story beige stucco building hard by the beach at the edge of town. "Golfing Visitors Welcome," says the sign under the eaves of the roof. I was changing my shoes in the parking lot when a small blue car arrived and a short man with a round face, silver-rimmed glasses, and a halo of white hair stepped out.

"Rev. Ferguson?" I asked.

"Yes, yes," he said, smiling. "Call me David."

Our playing partners hadn't arrived yet, and David suggested that we have a bite to eat and something to drink while we waited. We entered the clubhouse, which contains a small locker room and what was once advertised as a "gents' section," the equivalent of the men's grill in an American club. Nowadays women and men both use it. It has a bar, a pool table, a pinball machine, and a window looking out toward the first tee. We got sandwiches wrapped in cellophane. I ordered a Diet Coke, the pre-golf beverage of choice among my middle-aged compatriots. David asked for a half-pint of Belhaven cream ale. We sat down. He looked at my drink and told me a story, offering it, perhaps, as a kind of homily.

He was playing golf in Binghamton, New York. David, as it happened, had played quite a bit of golf in the States on exchange visits arranged between ministers of the Church of Scotland and ministers of American Presbyterian churches. This particular round was at the En-Joie Golf Club in Binghamton, site of the PGA Tour's BC Open.

It was a brutally hot summer day, ninety-five degrees, and David was quite thirsty as he and his partners made the turn. His hosts ordered "blends," which seemed to be a mixture of lemonade and orange juice. David had one. It went down easily and seemed quite refreshing. He had another. A few holes later he got another from a young lady riding around the course in a drinks cart, an amenity all but unknown on Scottish links.

David's golf got as hot as the weather. He played the back nine in 37 strokes and recorded a 79. It was a memorable round for a golfer who at his best has played "off fifteen," as the Scots say when asked about their handicaps. As it ended, he remarked to his partner that he had felt unusually relaxed over the ball.

"You should be relaxed," the partner said. "You've had three double vodkas."

David smiled at the memory and took a sip of his ale.

"Helped your game?" I asked.

"Yes, yes," he said.

Our playing partners arrived: the Rev. George Rollo, minister of St. Giles Church in Elgin, and Ian Bryce, a retired businessman who was treasurer of the church in Cullen. George was a genial man with thinning salt-and-pepper hair. Ian was red-haired and fair. We went outside and chose partners. It would be Ian and I against George and David. We dispensed with handicaps. "I'm your handicap," Ian said, grinning.

They all strapped their bags onto pull carts, which the Scots call trolleys. Cullen Golf Club had no powered golf carts of the sort that Americans so often ride in. Neither did any other course I saw in Scotland. Golf, in its homeland, was strictly a walking game.

We waited while a few boys teed off in front of us. They had their baseball caps on backward, and they wore jeans. They grounded their balls off the tee. They seemed to be having a fine time.

It was not hard to perceive, or at least to imagine, the hand of Old Tom Morris in what I could see of the Cullen course. As at the Old Course in St. Andrews, the first and eighteenth holes at Cullen shared a broad, flat fairway, with the sea to the golfer's right as he began the course and an old railway on the left. As at St. Andrews, a road bisected this fairway. At St. Andrews it was called Granny Clark's Wynd. At Cullen it was just a nameless track once used by fishermen hauling things to and from the beach of Cullen Bay. At both courses the arrangement meant that a round started gently. It was nearly impossible to miss the fairway from the first tee. At Cullen a player would have to hit almost sideways to find the beach or the Three Kings rocks.

A look at the card suggested that Cullen had other peculiarities. Par was 63, and the course stretched to only four thousand, six hundred and ten yards. Obviously, that was as much golf as could be accommodated on this bit of links land. The map on the card suggested that even to get this much in, the designers had had to have a few holes cross one another. The line of the ninth lay across and perpendicular to the lines of the eighth and tenth. The shot from the sixteenth tee had to cross the fifteenth fairway. And, of course, players on the first and eighteenth had to look out for one another as they played their respective holes. Had an American course been so designed, I suspect that personal injury lawyers would have been renting space in the clubhouse for branch offices. But in Scotland it was just part of the game. Holes crossed and shared greens at St. Andrews. They did so at Cullen.

It was our turn to play. I managed to hit a decent drive toward the road. So did Ian and George. David had a peculiar grip, with his hands about two inches apart on the shaft. It was, he explained, the way he'd felt comfortable when he took up the game. He'd had a few lessons since then, but no pro had ever persuaded him to change it. He hit a low fade about two hundred yards down the fairway.

David's was far from the only idiosyncratic swing I would see in Scotland. Many Scots, it seems, taught themselves the game and play it with unique styles that would horrify an American teaching pro. But most Scottish courses lack prac-

tice tees, and I never saw the Scottish equivalent of that standard sight next to an American clubhouse, the row of practicing golfers working on their form, at the end of which stand
a couple of pros giving lessons, imparting orthodox mechanics to eager students. The Scots just step onto the tee and play.

As we walked down the first fairway, eyeing the golfers
playing in on the eighteenth, I asked George where and
when he'd taken up the game.

It was, he said, at the University of St. Andrews, where he'd
studied divinity. Students at the university had ready and in-
expensive access to the St. Andrews courses. His superiors in
the ministry had encouraged him to learn the game.

Was that so he'd be able to socialize with the members of
his future congregations?

George smiled. "No, it was so I'd be able to get away from
them," he said.

He explained that the leaders of the Church of Scotland
felt it was important for ministers to have a hobby that got
them away from their desks, into the fresh air, that provided
exercise, that gave them a way to relieve the stress of their oc-
cupation.

We hit our shots to the first green, a small patch of closely
cropped turf nestled between the road and a ramp that led
upward to the second level of the links. None of us hit the
target, and in the end I was the only one to get up and down.
Ian and I were one up.

The second hole at Cullen was nowhere to be seen. The
second tee was visible, next to the ramp. But the tee pointed
us straight toward the face of a cliff perhaps fifty feet high.
Atop the cliff there was a black-and-white pole. The scorecard said the second was a one-hundred-and-thirty-yard par
three.

"Aim over the pole," David said. "But don't go too far.
There's a burn behind the green."

The wind off the firth seemed to be freshening. I had no
idea how to calculate the impact of a fifty-foot rise on club

selection, though the wind seemed to be worth about a club. I chose a nine-iron, hit it solidly, and watched it disappear over the directional pole.

"Might be too much," David said.

I waited for the rest of the group to hit. Then we trudged up the ramp to the upper level. George, it turned out, had hit the green. I was in the burn, a shallow little drainage ditch. I dropped and made four. George two-putted for a three. The match was even.

Walking down the next fairway, I told George that the second hole had reminded me, in spirit at least, of the Old Course at St. Andrews, where it seems that golfers are forever hitting blind tee shots and then waiting to discover whether their balls have found fairway or disaster.

George nodded. "I liked the New Course at St. Andrews better," he said. "I thought the Old Course had too many freaky bounces. It's unfair. I think golf should be fair."

It was an iconoclastic remark, since the New Course is generally considered inferior to the Old. Combined with David's unorthodox grip, it reminded me to ask about the role of the individual in Calvinist thought and Scottish culture.

"There's a historical tension within the Church of Scotland," George replied. "On the one hand, you have the notion of the priesthood of all believers, the idea that everyone has individual access to God. On the other hand, you have the establishment by Calvin of a religious city and state [Geneva]."

In the immediate aftermath of the Reformation and the founding of the Church of Scotland in the sixteenth century, the idea of the church dictating beliefs and behavior to individuals was clearly paramount, George said. The ancient records of his church, St. Giles, were replete with instances of Elginites being punished for drunkenness and fornication. Those were roughly the years when golfers were punished in Cullen, St. Andrews, and other towns for playing on Sunday.

We completed the third, a long par three, which I won

with a par. We went to the fourth tee, which resembled the second. We faced a cliffside with a directional pole mounted at the top. The green lay above the cliff on the third tier of the links, a short iron away. We hit the blind shots. David's barely made the top of the cliff. The rest disappeared in the direction, we hoped, of the flag.

George and I continued to chat about individualism as we trudged up the path to the fourth green and fifth tee. David took another path, a more abrupt climb up the face of the slope, which would lead more directly to his ball.

Over time, George said, the emphasis on imposed discipline in the Church of Scotland had waned. The emphasis on the role of the individual in setting his own spiritual course had increased. Nowadays the Church dictated very little. Sabbatarianism, the compulsory observance of the Sabbath, had waned in the twentieth century, though vestiges, like the closing of the Old Course at St. Andrews on Sundays, remained.

We got to the green, which sloped sharply toward the tee. George was above the hole and I was below. We waited for David. And waited some more. It occurred to all three of us at about the same time that David should have appeared at the top of the cliff. We went over and peered down.

David was making his way up the trail. "Had some trouble with my trolley," he said cheerily. "The bag kept falling off."

"It's a good thing you didn't have a heart attack," George greeted him. "Or we'd have had to carry you for fourteen holes."

Though George was closest to the hole, I had the advantage of an uphill putt. I made par. His birdie putt rolled well past the hole, and he missed the putt coming back for a bogey.

"Hard luck," David and Ian said. This was what they always said when someone missed a putt. It seemed to do little to console George.

We hit our tee shots down the fairway at the fifth, at three hundred and sixty yards the longest par four on the course.

Walking toward the balls, we resumed our discussion of Calvinism and individuality.

"Calvin was opposed to pleasure," David said. "But he never conquered human nature. The poet Robert Burns favored pleasure, and he was hauled before the session and accused of fornication. But the church couldn't stop him. Just as it couldn't stop people from golfing."

Was there a relationship between the two, I asked.

George grimaced, still thinking, perhaps, of that three-putt on No. 4.

"The way I'm playing it, golf is a poor substitute for fornication," he said.

We halved the fifth and then faced the sixth, a par three of one hundred and seventy-five yards. The land to our left fell seventy feet straight down to the lower tier of the course, and the shot to the green had to carry over an indentation in the cliff. It was a fine hole. I hit a far-less-than-fine shot that failed to carry the indentation. George was off the green by perhaps thirty feet with his first, but he confidently putted the ball close and made his par. This was a shot all the Scottish golfers I met had in their repertoire. Around the greens, golf in Scotland is a game of rolling your ball. The turf is low and lies are tight. The wind plays with shots in the air. Whenever I hit a lob around a Scottish green, my companions would call it an American shot. Usually it was ineffective.

We moved to the seventh tee, perhaps the most spectacular on the course. We were standing on the edge of the cliff. To the right lay Moray Firth. Immediately below us, gulls and terns were circling lazily around the huge red crags that dotted the lower portion of the course. The hole lay some two hundred and ten yards out and seventy feet down. Just beyond it, a small burn trickled toward the sea.

George, with the honor, hit a wide shot that disappeared in some thick grass. "Oh, well," he said. "This will help my handicap against the Anglicans."

I hit my shot toward the green and was lucky when it

stopped in the narrow patch of turf between the green and the burn. As we walked, cautiously and single file, down the path that wound toward the lowland, I asked about his reference to the Anglicans.

There was an annual competition between twelve-member teams of clerics from the Church of Scotland and clerics from the Church of England, David explained. One summer it would be held in Scotland and the next in England. "It's no big thing," he said. "The main qualification is knowing the captain of your team." Both he and George had represented the Church of Scotland in summers past.

Apparently, the Scots had long suspected the English of inflating their handicaps. David recalled in particular one match when a Scottish minister, playing off seven, had finished the sixth hole three down to his English opponent. The Anglican, despite playing off sixteen, had made nothing but pars. The Scot walked off the course, enraged. He was required to apologize to the members of both teams before he was allowed to play again.

George, meanwhile, used the issue to find some solace when he seemed on the verge of putting a large number on his scorecard.

I won the seventh. Fortunately, the match ahead of us had accelerated and we did not have to worry about golfers on the ninth hole crossing the path of our drives off the eighth tee or golfers going down ten crossing under the shots we hit toward the ninth green.

We made the turn under the brow of a massive promontory that marked the western boundary of the course. The wind off the sea changed, from an accommodating right-to-left breeze that helped keep fades on line, to what seemed like a left-to-right gale that threatened to turn even good shots into catastrophic slices. Or so I told myself after I hit my tee shot on the tenth into deep grass on the right and lost it. David, playing his consistent low fade with his split grip, pitched onto the green and made his par to win the hole.

We turned into the strangest part of the Cullen links, a stretch of four consecutive par threes that wound their way among the crags. The eleventh played two-hundred-and-fifteen yards to the foot of Boar Crag, a red stone pile large enough to have had a cave drilled into it by the RAF during World War II for ammunition storage.

The way to play it, David explained, was not to aim at the green, which was small and hard to hold. The ideal shot, rather, was aimed toward the markers for the twelfth tee, which lay just above the beach. This ideal shot bounced around in some hummocks and swales below those tees and trickled down to the green.

I couldn't manage that shot, couldn't bring myself to aim out over the beach, which was out-of-bounds. I aimed just a little left of the flag. The wind and the terrain carried my shot down into a hollow well below the putting surface. I made bogey and we lost another hole.

The twelfth, a par three of one hundred and eighty yards, was nearly a blind shot. The player stood with his back to the firth and Boar Crag on his left. He aimed at a directional pole stuck in a hillside about one hundred and thirty yards inland. The green and flag were just beyond it. I hit a four-iron over the marker. David, standing ten yards to my left at the very foot of the Boar Crag, could see a bit of the green and flag.

"Hard luck," he announced. "Hit the green and spun off."

Another hole gone.

The thirteenth at Cullen was completely blind. Standing on the tee, the golfer looked straight at the face of Red Crag, maybe fifty feet high. A yellow arrow was painted on the top of the crag, pointing the way to the green, which was on the other side. You hit an eight-iron over the arrow and then waited until you walked around to the other side of the crag to find out if you'd hit the green.

The fourteenth completed this quirky stretch. It was a two-hundred-yard hole, back toward the sea, that was partly blind.

The tee shot had to skirt the edge of Boar Crag to fir
green. By the time we putted out, Ian and I were two down.

"Cullen produces a lot of good iron players," David observed.

The implication was that someone who could regularly
play those four holes in par, in varying wind conditions, had
to be very sharp with those clubs.

That called to mind what MacDonald had written about
the preferability of a life of interest over a life of ease. Interest,
rather than ease, seemed to be the leitmotiv of the stretch of
holes we'd just played.

Ian and I badly needed to rally as we teed off on the fifteenth, Cullen's long hole, a par five of five hundred and fifteen yards heading back to the clubhouse. With acres of open
ground to my right and the wind from the sea pushing balls in
that direction, I somehow managed to hook my drive left into
the tall grass near the top of the dunes that separated the links
from the beach. David and George both hit useful drives into
the hummocky fairway.

As we looked for my ball and I pondered the inherent interest in the way a ball unerringly finds the unlikeliest trouble, I asked David and George what they thought of
MacDonald's thesis.

"Well," said David, "from the Reformation onward, our
education has been cerebral and practical. The list of Scottish
musicians is nil. We have one great Scottish poet, Burns. But
look at the long list of engineers and inventions we have—
the telephone, macadam, television, the steam engine. Wher-
ever the Scot goes, he's well received because he's not afraid
to build practical things. The English were administrators. We
wanted to know how things worked."

"I'm still trying to figure out how the golf swing works,"
George grumbled. "But Scots do have an ethic that it's better
to be doing something rather than watching."

David found my ball and I hacked it out of the tall grass. I
had no chance to reach the green with my third and settled

for sending it down to the left of the rounded hillock that guarded the green, a hillock the size and shape of the *kurgani,* or burial mounds, in which the nomads of the Asian steppe placed their dead. Given that David and George played confidently down the fairway and were about to go dormie three, it seemed an apt symbol for Ian and me. The sun chose that moment to break through the low gray clouds that had covered the sky all afternoon, bathing the course in bright light. It seemed to be gently mocking me.

"Hard luck," David murmured as my thirty-foot, desperation par putt missed the hole by a couple of feet.

David and George were the kindest of competitors. I owed that, in part, to George's presence, David told me. We hit our drives toward the sixteenth hole, the first of three par four finishing holes that tacked back toward the clubhouse along the flat, green, opening plain of the links and were among the least interesting holes on the course. David was himself not always above a little gamesmanship, he told me.

There had been a time during a four-ball match at another course when he thought that one of his opponents was trying to "wind us up." This fellow was the type who always managed to comment on how rotten David's luck had been, how tough his lie was, how difficult it would be for him to select a club. Finally, on the sixteenth hole, as both lay near the green in two shots, David had had enough.

"Tell me," David inquired of his opponent as they walked toward the green, "do you believe in God?"

Startled, the man averred that, yes, he did.

"Do you go to church on Sundays?" David continued.

Now the man was a bit irritated and a bit unnerved. He wasn't sure what that had to do with golf, he said.

"Well," David persisted, "do you have a personal relationship with the Lord?"

That was hitting close to the man's presumably troubled conscience. He mumbled something indistinct in reply.

"Well, I do," David said. "And I am going to get up and down!"

David hit his chip. It rolled in the cup. His opponent, completely unnerved, bladed his chip across the green and lost the hole.

On the next tee the man looked nervously at David. "You're not going to talk like that again, are you?"

"No, I don't think so," David said.

And he didn't. He didn't have to. His sinful opponent, now completely off his game, lost the last two holes and the match.

I said that I was easily sinner enough to make me vulnerable to the same ploy, should David try it.

"Oh, I couldn't do that now," he said. "George would laugh at me."

Spared an examination of conscience, I parred the next two holes. George and David, suffering either from fatigue or generosity, bogeyed them. Ian and I were still alive as we drove our balls down the eighteenth fairway. Clouds scudded through the sky, making the sunlight patchy. Bits of the bay were glittering. The Three Kings were in shade. We sorted our balls out from those driven down the same patch of grass by the match playing off the first tee.

I had not, I realized, discovered anything definitive about the Scottish character during this round in Cullen. No doubt a scientist would have told me that the very notion of a national character was a dubious proposition, given the vast diversity of personality types within a given population.

Still, I thought there was some connection between golf and certain common Scottish traits like individualism and industriousness, like the preference for a life of interest over a life of ease. That connection, I suspect, helped to explain why golf had taken root in lands populated by Scottish immigrants while it remained basically an exogenous game in cultures with different traditions, such as those of Iran and the rest of the Islamic world. I do not mean to say that Muslims, or other people who believe in placing the tenets of their religion above their own judgment, cannot play golf and play it well. They can. Nor do I wish to suggest that other factors, like climate and wealth, do not play a role in the popularity of golf in a given country. Of course, they do. I simply suggest that certain cultural attributes can help create a propitious environment for golf.

A skeptic might point to the countries of the Far East, particularly Japan and Korea. Golf, once exogenous there, has taken root and flourished, even though Scottish influence on those societies is, at most, indirect. Those countries, though, share a Taoist philosophical tradition that has some key points in common with a religious tradition that proclaims the priesthood of all believers.

"The sage does not expect that others use his criteria as their own," the *Tao Te Ching* says, meaning that every individual has to find his or her own path to enlightenment through discipline and meditation.

Spoken like a golfer.

We hit our approach shots to Cullen's eighteenth. Mine was twenty feet away. David and George were off the green. We walked toward the hole in a state of pleasant fatigue, thinking about the clubhouse and the comforts within.

Of one thing I was certain. I had yet to play golf with a dour Scot. Golf for the people of Cullen was neither grim nor uncomfortable. It was a pleasure as welcome as the sunshine when it broke through the clouds.

David and George chipped up and, being good hosts, missed their par putts. I sank mine to halve the match.

"Yes, yes," David said.

The Fellowship of the Links

All masculine games are contests.

—Haultain

It's the last Thursday in January, a workday. At home people are struggling to their offices through frosty streets clogged with traffic. I am not among them. Instead, I am sitting in a van at an airport in Florida with eleven other men. We are going to play golf in an annual competition called the Groundhog Cup. I am trying to figure out why. And I am pondering the place of camaraderie among the pleasures of the game.

There is no doubt that the company one keeps distinguishes golf from other sports. As Dr. Lichtenberg had pointed out, golfers don't necessarily oppose one another, the way tennis players or boxers must. They are all, in a sense, on the same side, battling against the difficulties of the game. And I know of few activities in which groups of strangers may meet at a starting point, spend four or five companionable hours together regardless of age, sex, or skill, and part as, if not friends, at least pleasant acquaintances. I am the sort of golfer who decides now and again to play on the spur of the moment. I show up unannounced at a golf course, like Blanche DuBois, dependent on the kindness of strangers. The strangers I have met at golf courses have never disappointed me.

But this weekend is not about a pickup game with strangers or even acquaintances at a club. This weekend is about golfing camaraderie of another sort.

The van, dispatched to meet us by Innisbrook, the resort that is graciously relieving us of several hundred dollars a day for the privilege of playing on its fairways, lurches into motion. Reconnaissance gets underway. Someone spots the first palm tree. Someone else spots people wearing shorts.

I open the book I've been reading on the plane—*In the Shadow of Man,* Jane Goodall's classic observation of chimpanzees in the Gombe Stream Reserve in Tanzania. "There is a great deal in chimpanzee social behavior to remind us of some of our own behavior," Goodall writes. "More, perhaps, than many of us would care to admit."

Hmm . . . Goodall is only one of many sources I have seen recently suggesting that a cigar may be more than a cigar, that men are not fully aware of their motivations—and that simple friendship and shared love of the game don't adequately describe the ties that bind golfers. Among certain non-golfers, it is an article of faith that the golf course is not what it seems to be, that it is in truth the locus of a vast cabal, the Ravenite Social Club of a mafia that illegitimately runs the world. *The New York Times,* in a recent article about the social clubs of the black upper class, compared them to country clubs, "where golf is the pretext and making business connections is the subtext." It wasn't necessary for the writer to cite a source or any evidence for this statement. He simply had to state it. In the minds of the *Times*'s editors, it fell into the category of obvious truths, like the fact that the sun rises in the east and that the word *network* is a verb. No documentation was needed.

I realize that customer golf exists. But suggesting that business connections are the underlying purpose of golf is rather like suggesting that people go to church on Sundays to show off their new clothes. It may be true in some cases, but it misses the central point.

Based on the networking theory, I suppose a typical conversation among Groundhog Cup contestants would go like this:

> *Joe: Nice drive, bud. Oh, by the way, there's a guy I played with last week looking for a job. Know of anything?*
> *Bill: Why, we're looking for a vice president for marketing right now! What's his handicap?*

That doesn't sound like what I hear around me. The contestants in the Groundhog Cup all make a living, of course. A couple of our number sell stocks. One builds houses. Another demolishes buildings. One's a painting contractor and another does drywall. We have a man who assesses risks for investors in foreign economies and another who makes false teeth for dentists. But we aren't talking about that this morning in the Innisbrook van and, in my recollection, almost never do. Instead, we are deeply engaged in the ritual pre-tournament trashing of one another's handicaps.

"Kelso, what's that down around your feet?" Barnyard calls out. Kelso looks down and sees, of course, only the floor of the van.

"Looked like sand," Barnyard continues. "Looked like your sandbag sprung a leak." Kelso, whose handicap rose inexplicably from six to eleven last year, blushes and protests his innocence. He really deserves an eleven handicap, he says. He needs it.

"Right, Kelso," I join in. "You're the most shameless hustler since Monica Lewinsky."

"No, what about you?" Barnyard needles. "I hear you've been out practicing your short game again. You shouldn't be an eleven. Ought to be a nine!"

I blush because I have indeed stolen a few hours in the past week to visit our nearly frozen home course, chipping and putting with numb fingers, getting ready for this event.

And so it goes. As the asphalt rumbles beneath the van and one Florida condo–office–mall starts to seem like another and I begin to have faith that the sun is not going to disappear and it's not going to rain on our first day, I turn again to Goodall's observation of chimpanzees.

"At least once a week, the Gombe males, usually in groups of not less than three, visit the peripheral areas of their community range," Goodall writes.

Obviously, there's no resemblance to us Groundhog Cuppers in that. We don't have a community range, and we get away like this once or twice a year, not once a week. In my case, at least, this is a function of the enlightened self-interest of my wife, who has learned that giving her blessing to a few days of golf in the sun at the end of January can prevent a few weeks of crankiness in February and March, when it seems like spring and the new golf season will never come to Maryland.

The van pulls off the highway and into the resort, discharging us, pale and blinking, before the reception building at Innisbrook. This is a little bit like loading a bunch of very thirsty derelicts into a bus and letting them off at a liquor store, armed with a hundred dollars. They are happy to be there but a trifle uncertain about where to start.

Innisbrook is perhaps six hundred acres of prime alligator habitat transformed into four golf courses, several pools, a few restaurants, and clusters of low-rise condos with golfish names like Dornoch and Royal Aberdeen. At this time of year, the resort processes hordes of visiting golfers, shepherding them with great efficiency around the grounds in vans driven by friendly retirees from back north. The Groundhog Cuppers are struck nearly silent by the array of temptations they can see. First tees. Fairways. Putting greens. Driving ranges. Practice balls. Even practice bunkers. We've been without golf long enough that it seems like it might be pleasant to take a bag of those range balls into the practice bunker and spend an hour or so sharpening up that sand game.

I scan the competition. Like boys on a playground, most of us go by nicknames. There's the Bug, my roommate for the next few days, an amiable ringer for an old cartoon character named Baby Huey. The Rocket is down the hall. He's short, volatile. When he's playing well, his "Yee-ha" cries can be heard two fairways away. When he's not, his scowl could set fire to dry underbrush. L.T., gray-maned and intense, looks like he could be headed for a golf course or a convention of Harley-Davidson riders.

The nicknames rarely reflect either character or appearance. Barnyard, contrary to the connotations of the name, is in fact the most elegant and natty member of the group (although that is not a difficult distinction to earn). Kelso, the accused sandbagger, has neither the high-strung temperament nor the fragile body of the eponymous thoroughbred. He's stocky, friendly, and far too honest to have a questionable handicap. He's got a kink in his swing rhythm and a kind heart.

Maybe, I catch myself thinking, that kink and that kind heart will be his downfall.

The overriding purpose of male chimp life, Goodall writes, is to establish a hierarchy at the top of which sits the alpha male. Male chimps compete for alphahood almost incessantly. They make their fur stand on end and look fierce. They tear branches from trees and shake them about like weapons. Sometimes they actually fight one another. But they prefer to establish their places in the hierarchy with as little physical risk as possible, by blustering rather than bludgeoning. The rise of the chimp named Mike, who learned to intimidate his peers by banging together empty kerosene canisters, was but a variation on this theme.

The alpha male chimp has dibs on the finer things of

chimp life—bananas and females. When Goodall left bananas at a feeding station, she observed that the alpha male ate his fill before the others could have any. When one of the females came into estrus, the alpha male satisfied himself before the other males got a turn. Life for the non-alpha males seemed to be lived with an eye cast back over their shoulders, sneaking food and sneaking sex when the alpha's attention was elsewhere.

Goodall found that she didn't have to observe the chimps feeding or mating to figure out the hierarchy. The status of each chimp was evident in the way he greeted the others. "A greeting between two chimps nearly always re-establishes the dominance status of one relative to another," she wrote. When a chimp meets another of higher status, he assumes a position looking up at the individual he is greeting. He bows rapidly, almost bobbing. And he emits a sequence of sounds that ethologists like Goodall describe as "pant-grunting."

Well, I think. No one's pant-grunting around here. There's plenty of food for everyone, including bananas. The only females about seem to be waitresses in the restaurant, and they look like they'd be happy to take a tray and decapitate any golfer who got fresh enough to use the word *estrus*. When Goodall wrote about similarities between human behavior and chimp behavior, she must have been thinking of some other group besides golfers. No one I can see seems to be after alpha status.

What we do seem to be after is each other's money. Everyone in the Groundhog Cup tosses sixty dollars into a communal pot. Half the money is distributed every day to the best net scores. The other half goes into a purse for the overall leaders after three days. Then there are the Nassaus and side bets that go on within each foursome, especially in the afternoon rounds, which are not part of the Cup competition. Our wagering is petty by the standards of some groups I have heard about. But it is taken very seriously.

In fact, I have been on a lot of golf outings with different groups. I have never been on one where everyone agreed to play just for fun and camaraderie. There is always a bet. The amounts are never large enough to change anyone's credit rating or threaten a mortgage payment. They're symbolic. But they seem to be as necessary to this kind of event as a pocket full of tees and a fresh sleeve of balls.

My own bets start to look more promising after the warm-up round on Thursday afternoon. We play this on Innisbrook's Island course, and our first tee shot, off the tenth hole as it happens, must carry a sizable lagoon. This isn't the easiest shot for a group of players who just stepped off the plane and haven't been able to hit a ball for a couple of months. But for reasons unknown, my good swing decides to make its appearance at this juncture. My drive flies long and straight, into the distant fairway. Maybe, I think, lack of practice is what I need.

In fact, I hit the ball reasonably well all afternoon, and only a few sand hiccups prevent me from breaking 80. (I really should have gone to that practice bunker.) I collect a few dollars in Nassau bets. At dinner Barnyard turns his needle on me again, proclaiming me the favorite despite my long history of failure in these competitions.

I am still waiting to hear conversation about business connections, that subtext the writer in the *Times* spoke of. But there is none. Mainly we talk about the loops in our swings, the cricks in our backs, and the condition of Innisbrook's greens. This is fairly standard. I once made a list of the discussion topics I heard this group take up during the course of a day's golfing. Here it is:

—Number of miles to the course.
—The price of gasoline.
—The economics of owning a gas station.
—Number of minutes left in the trip to the course.
—The stakes in the match.
—The vagaries of the game, including how easy it is to

make bogeys, tricky greens, and the fragility of a hot streak.

—The rudeness of bringing cell phones onto the course.

—The profitability of betting against someone who's trying to play golf and talk on the phone at the same time.

—The extreme profitability of betting against someone who is talking on the cell phone with a woman other than his wife.

—Sex with two women at the same time.

—Golf courses you want to play so badly that you'd give up the opportunity to participate in a sexual threesome if that were the only available tee time.

—What people shot when they had a chance to play Pine Valley.

—What locker room attendants expect in tips.

I was glad I wasn't selling the original cast recording from that day. It would have been unutterably boring to someone not playing golf.

My own theory about golf and camaraderie has to do with the atomization of contemporary society and the way males are raised. Few of us, I suspect, live the way earlier societies lived, and the way the male chimps of the Gombe Stream live, in the lifelong proximity of the same people. We may grow up in one place, though many do not. We generally get our higher education in another place. Our careers take us to several additional places. We reach midlife with our close friends scattered around the country. How many of us still know where our best friends from grade school live, let alone spend time with them?

Perhaps if this were not the case, males would have a different social web. It might be based on a long, shared history of school and work; of shared friends; of shared battles against floods, droughts, and enemy tribes; of thoughts about the same songs and poetry. If this were so, we might talk to one another differently.

Instead, we have sport. From the time we are old enough to run, we are taught to come together with our peers to play games. We continue to do so as adults. Games give us something to do with one another. Women, I have noticed, have other devices to bring them together. They might, for example, belong to a book club. They get together to discuss a book they've all read, recreating the literature seminar. Men recreate the playground. We get together to play golf.

On Friday morning, the first day of formal Groundhog Cup competition, with the sun but a gray smudge on the eastern horizon, I begin playing quite well. I par the first hole. On the second, a short par four, I hit my sand wedge about a foot from the pin and make birdie. I do some quick calculations, blissfully disregarding Bob Rotella's advice about keeping your thoughts on the shot at hand. If I can keep up this pace, I'll finish fifty-four holes at twenty-seven under par. Add in my handicap strokes, and my net score will be sixty under. That, I think, should do quite well. In fact, it would beat last year's winning net by something like seventy strokes.

Of course, this fantasy soon collapses. On the third, a short par five, I hit my approach a little thin and skull it over the back of the green. I chip too hard, three-putt, and take double bogey. I hit the green on the next hole, a long par three. But I completely misread the break on my seventy-foot putt, leaving myself twenty feet from the hole. My second putt stops three feet short. And my third putt rims around the hole and slides out, taunting me. I leave the green muttering darkly about pin positions, course design, and my own feckless putting. At this pace I'll finish fifty-hour holes fifty-four over par.

I go through the round putting abominably. I find myself wishing I were putting well enough to call it yippy. The Bug, who is part of today's foursome, is talking about grain on the greens as if he were Johnny Miller. I'll leave a fifteen-foot putt three feet short, and he'll stroke his chin and say, " 'Gainst the grain, huh? Where's the setting sun?" This begins to irritate me, considering that both Bug and I have about as much chance of reading grain as we have of reading cuneiform.

And I am not the only one irritated. Around the course, in my own foursome and in others nearby, I can hear the sounds of bile rising: the dreaded hollow thwock as a golf ball strikes a pine tree; the yet more dreaded thwock-thwock-thwock as it penetrates into the deep woods and bounces around in there; a quiet splash as another finds a swamp; low, muttered curses around the greens on the front side; loud, unmuffled curses around the greens on the back side.

By the eighteenth hole my game is tattered, and I come nowhere close to the green in the requisite two strokes. My pitch on is sloppy, and I have a twenty-footer to salvage par. The putt looks like it needs to follow the line of a small ridge running along the right side of the green and then curl into the cup.

I look toward the sky and mutter, "Okay, God. Payback time." I don't actually believe that God intervenes much in the affairs of men. And I don't really believe that my putting travails on this brilliantly sunny, warm morning amount to the trials of Job. Still, I somehow feel that I am owed something. And feeling that way, I curl the ball into the hole.

It's a fortuitous par, though all it gives me for the day is an 85. My fellow Groundhog Cuppers, I will learn at lunch, have had even more trouble with their winter-encrusted games than I have, and my net 74 is the best of the day by a stroke. When I pocket the prize for the day's best round, I have to stifle an urge to leave Innisbrook immediately, find a church, and stuff all the money in a poor box.

• • •

Chimps, Goodall writes, almost invariably follow a display of alpha striving with a display of reconciliation. No matter which chimp wins the bluster showdown, the winner and loser usually wind up sitting next to each other, picking the bugs, thorns, and other annoyances of jungle life out of their pelts.

We, of course, are not chimps, and our morning's competition does not lead to any mutual fur grooming. In fact, by evening mere human camaraderie seems to be dissipating. By tacit consent the whole group does not gather for dinner. Individuals stay at the range till dark, trying to cobble together a swing or a putting stroke, even though they have already played thirty-six holes of golf. They watch their competitors out of the corners of their eyes. They eat dinner in twos and threes. They go to bed early.

The next morning we start on the tenth hole of the Island course, the same course we played for our warm-up round on Thursday afternoon. But something is different. When I look across the lagoon to the fairway down which I so skillfully smacked the ball on Thursday, the green opening between the trees looks about as big as a keyhole. I try to conjure up the visual image of my ball soaring straight and far, but in my mind's eye this morning, imaginary balls seem to want to end up in imaginary lagoons. I push my drive weakly into the trees on the right.

That shot is emblematic of the way things will go in the second round. I can't drive the ball straight. I can't putt. In between I'm not doing too well, either. My game has fallen apart faster than Yugoslavia. My emotions run from befuddlement to irritation, to anger, to horror, and finally, to amusement. By the seventh hole I am somewhere in the neighborhood of fourteen over par for the day, working assiduously on losing my third golf ball, and starting to laugh at myself.

I can think of two theories to account for this poor play. The first is that God has decided to punish me for my blasphemous remark on the final green in the first round. This hypothesis is instinctively satisfying, placing me and my golf game somewhere close to the center of the universe. But it begs the question of whether the Supreme Being would indeed look on indifferently as human beings slaughtered one another by the carload throughout this century, then take the time to wreak vengeance on a vacationing golfer who demanded (spitefully and impertinently, I admit) divine help in rolling a ball into a hole.

Despite this theological flaw, I find this hypothesis more appealing than the only alternative I can come up with, which is that as soon as I found out I was leading the Groundhog Cup, I started to choke like a dog.

Barnyard, who is part of my foursome this morning, has meanwhile begun to play well. He's got his game face on— grim, determined, intense. He's found his rhythm and his touch, and he's reeled off several consecutive pars.

On the ninth tee I do something cowardly, despicable, and unsportsmanlike. I compliment him.

"You're really playing well," I say as innocently as I can. "I think you're going to win this thing."

With those words still warm in his ears, Barnyard steps up to the ball. Our ninth hole (the course's eighteenth) is a tight, nasty little par four, a dogleg with a wooded swamp on the right and water on the left side of the fairway. He hits it into the woods right. He can't find his ball. He drops one. He hits that one into the pond in front of the green. He drops another and hits it into the water as well. Leaving the green with a nine on his card, he no longer looks like he is going to win.

This, I think, is yet another bit of evidence demonstrating the patent foolishness of Goodall's contention that human behavior is similar to chimp behavior. When chimps get close to what they want, they seize it. Boldly. Gracefully. Confidently. When one of the Groundhog Cuppers gets close to what he wants, he hits a ball into the water.

When the round is over, I have a score that is barely in double digits. But the amazing thing is that I am still, as Johnny Miller would say, in the hunt. Collectively, the Groundhog Cup field has limped into the clubhouse for lunch looking like Washington's army in the depths of the winter at Valley Forge. No one has broken 90 for the round. I am only four strokes behind the Rocket, and I will be in the final foursome for the climactic third round on Sunday morning.

But there isn't much time to commiserate or to analyze our problems. We have to hustle over to the first tee of the Eagle's Watch course for our afternoon four-ball rounds. Of course, we play the back tees. Hey, we may not be able to break 90, but we're men. Eagle's Watch from the white tees measures only six thousand, one hundred yards. Men play six-thousand, five-hundred-yard golf courses.

Halfway through this round, still struggling with my swing, it occurs to me that there might be another explanation for our lousy golf. The competitive pressure is much lighter in the afternoon round, and yet my foursome is still hacking the ball around. So maybe it's not that we're chokers. Maybe we're all just a little too old to jump on a plane in January and start playing thirty-six holes a day. Maybe our bad swings have to do with fatigued muscles and sore backs.

Nah, I think. It couldn't be that we're getting old. It must be divine retribution.

When the round is over, I put aside thoughts of old age and heavenly wrath and head for the practice range. I have got to get back the swing I had when I got off the plane. While I'm at it, I need to do something about skulled pitches and stubbed chips, to say nothing of putting. The young man in the shack at the range looks at me with knowing eyes, the same eyes, I suspect, that junkies see when they get their methadone at the clinic. He hands me a couple of sacks of balls. It's dark before I decide I am through. A full moon—a blue moon on this last evening in January—is rising over the practice range.

The Bug is still out by the practice green. I can hear him working on sand shots, even though it's now too dark to see him very well. I walk over. He looks like a shadowy bear over there, half hidden behind a screen of trees, thrashing around.

"Ready for dinner, Bug?"

The Bug shrugs his big shoulders. He tries another practice blast, catches too much sand, and the ball barely trickles to the practice green, which by this time in the day is holding more golf balls than Titleist's warehouse. They look like a shadowy mosaic in the moonlight.

"Nah," he says. "Think I'll go down to the lighted end of the range and pull a . . ."

He hesitates, his fatigued brain presumably searching for the term *all-nighter,* unused since school days.

"A groin muscle?" I suggest helpfully.

The Bug smiles wanly. "Nah. I'm going to be like that pro from Fuji, what's-his-name."

"Vijay Singh," I prompt. From Fiji, not Fuji, but close enough.

"Yeah, that guy. Hits a lot of balls," the Bug says. "I'll be in to dinner later."

So I leave the range, feeling inadequate because after thirty-six holes and three bags of practice balls, I am too tired to go down to the lighted end of the practice range and keep digging in the dirt, hunting for the stroke Hogan promised is in there. The Bug, I think, is a better man than I am.

I go back to the room, take a shower, and pick up *In the Shadow of Man* again. Goodall is describing how a young chimp named Figan begins to make his way up the domination hierarchy among the males at the Gombe Stream Reserve. First Figan refuses to back down when the older chimps bluster and threaten him. Gradually he begins to bluster and intimidate them. When Figan turns his back on the threatening display of Mike, the alpha male, Goodall write., the end of Mike's reign is near. Figan is saying he's not afraid of Mike, that he's younger and stronger. Soon it is Figan who will be getting first dibs on bananas and females.

It seems very far away.

The chemistry of our own group has changed enough in the past day to cause everyone to gather again for dinner. The Bug, last off the golf course, makes it to the table in time for the second or third round of drinks. The Groundhog Cuppers this evening are displaying a kind of camaraderie. The bond among us perhaps resembles that of soldiers who have survived battle together. We are all still dazed and wounded from the shock of the morning's terrible golf.

Midway through the entree, our treasurer, Dougie, pays off the Rocket and the other top scorers of the day. None of them, I suspect, has ever before won anything for a net score in excess of 80. Then someone suggests that we ratchet the stakes a little higher with a Calcutta pool on the final results. (A Calcutta is an auction in which each contestant is bought by the highest bidder. When a winner emerges, the purchaser of the winner then collects the pooled money.) This proposal appeals to two Groundhog Cup constituencies. Those who are playing merely badly figure they might win and collect more money. Those who are playing atrociously figure this may be a way to recoup. If they can't win with their golf games, they might be able to win with astute handicapping.

So Buck, a Groundhog Cupper with sales experience, starts the bidding. He packages the last four players in the standings, and they go for ten dollars. The next few players bring twenty or thirty. Kelso and Barnyard each attract about seventy-five dollars. My turn comes. It's an odd moment. How much do I really like my own chances tomorrow?

I'm willing, I discover, to bid another sixty dollars on myself, matching the amount each of us contributed to the original Groundhog Cup purse. But that is not enough. My rights go for one hundred and thirty, to a player named Syl. It's ten bucks more than the Bug attracted. Maybe the others don't think his overtime practice will help him.

Finally, the Rocket goes on the block. He sits silently while the bidding gets up to two hundred and fifty. As Buck says, "going twice," the Rocket speaks. Two-sixty. There's an appreciative murmur around the table. The waitress brings another round of drinks.

The bidding continues. We've pushed past symbolic levels now, and there's a game of chicken afoot. The Rocket clearly wants to own himself tomorrow. Bidding against him may force him to overpay. But it could backfire if the Rocket decides to bail out and leave someone else owning him at an inflated price. There are a couple of intervening bids. The Rocket finally claims himself for a little more than three hundred dollars.

Over the rest of dinner, a secondary auction breaks out as the owners of various contenders sell a portion of their rights. I buy back half of myself from Syl. Syl, hedging his bets, buys a piece of the Rocket. By the time coffee is poured, the final round of the Groundhog Cup has more confusion and conflicts of interest than the craps table on Casino Night in the parish hall at St. Bridget's. If we had a commissioner, he'd be impeached.

Back at the room, the Bug and I are too tired to talk much. The Bug goes one up on the legend of Cool Papa Bell, the old Negro League ballplayer who was so fast he was said to be able to turn out the light and get into bed before it got dark in the room. The Bug is not only in bed but asleep before the light disappears.

The next morning, up before dawn, I part the curtains and peer out the window to check the pavement under the streetlight outside, looking for the gleam of puddles. No sign of rain. We dress quietly. I can hear the shoelaces scraping through the eyelets as I pull them tight.

I skip breakfast and head for the Copperhead course, Innisbrook's premier track, venue every December for the J.C.

Penney Classic, in which male and female pros play as teams in a best ball competition. And, of course, the traditional final round site for the Groundhog Cup.

I head for the practice green, which is swathed in mist rising from the ground as the sun appears over the eastern horizon. I open a new sleeve of Titleist Tour Balata 90s and mark them with an indelible pen—one dot, two dots, three dots. Then I roll putts, looking for a stroke, looking for some feel. On my first long putt, I miss by four feet and then miss the comeback. Not a good sign.

I go to the practice tee, where the rest of the Cuppers are warming up. Faces are tight. Mouths are pursed lines. The occasional "Good morning" and "Good luck" are muffled sounds, spoken through clenched teeth.

Finally it's time for the last foursome to tee off. The Rocket slowly swishes his driver. L.T. works a cramp out of his neck. The Bug walks up and peers down the first fairway, a fairway he's peered down at least half a dozen times before.

"So, this a par five?" The Bug asks.

"Shut the_____up and play golf, Bug," L.T. snaps, establishing the tone of warmth and fellowship that always distinguishes final round play in the Groundhog Cup.

The first on the Copperhead course is an exemplary starting hole for a resort, a shortish par five with an elevated tee and a generous fairway. It's designed to get play started pleasantly. This I barely manage to do. My drive is a weak, fading pop-up, but it's in the fairway and I am flooded with relief. I bogey the first two holes, but I tell myself they're adrenaline bogeys, caused by hitting my approach shots a little long and then chipping back too strongly.

I have a Jack Fleck experience on the third tee. It is not an odd feeling in the hands. It is more a sense of unaccustomed command over rhythm and timing. The third on the Copperhead is not a hole I have ever played well. It's a par four, four hundred and twenty yards, with a lake on the right side that threatens the drive and then has to be carried with the long approach to the green. But this time I manage a good drive down the right center and hit a four-iron onto the green for a routine par.

At the fourth, a par three, I hit a seven-iron to within five feet of the pin. My birdie putt slides past the hole, but I feel increasingly confident. At the fifth, a long par five, I sink a fifteen-foot birdie putt. At the sixth, a long and tough par four, I get up and down from a deep bunker in front of the green. When I par the seventh with a drive, an eight-iron, and two putts, I realize that I have played the first seven holes just a stroke over par.

The rest of the group are having the usual problems. The Rocket half-stubs a chip onto the seventh green, then stands forever over a three-foot bogey putt before leaving it short. He walks off the green glowering and silent, with a six.

It occurs to me that I am probably leading.

My reaction is predictable. I double-bogey the next three holes, giving the lead back to the Rocket. The engorged feeling in my throat doesn't fully dissipate until the twelfth tee.

The Bug, meanwhile, starts to make a move. He pars a couple of holes that the Rocket and I bogey and then steps onto the sixteenth tee. No. 16 at Copperhead is a daunting hole, a long dogleg right around a lake. Alligators often sun themselves on the lake's banks, occasionally giving rise to the question of how close a player is willing to stand to a seemingly somnolent gator in order to obey the injunction to play it as it lies. But the Bug has no fear. He starts his ball out over the water and draws it into the fairway forty yards ahead of my cautious fade.

I should've stayed out and practiced under the moon, I think. Maybe I'd be hitting draws like that.

I am two hundred yards out from the green. I take a four-wood and swing too hard. The divot I raise probably should've been accompanied by an environmental impact statement, large as it is and coming as it does in the immediate vicinity of a wetland. My ball rises weakly and settles about fifty yards ahead. The Bug then hits a gorgeous shot, covering the flag all the way and stopping perhaps five feet from the hole. He looks very likely to make a birdie.

I hit a seven-iron to fifteen feet and make the par putt, but it doesn't seem to matter. The Bug sinks his birdie putt.

"Bug, you birdie that hole, you deserve to win," I say.

L.T., himself out of it, bends over the scorecard and adds numbers while we wait to tee off on the seventeenth, a par three of one hundred and seventy five yards. He shakes his head, smiles. "You and Bug are tied," he says, mischievously I think. "Rocket's a stroke behind."

I take a deep breath and look around. The morning clouds have burned off, and the sky is a deep cerulean blue. A breeze ruffles the tops of the palm trees in the woods that line the hole. I pick up a little of the fragrant grass left by the mower and scatter it in the air. The wind is helping a little. I draw the four-iron from the bag and visualize a shot flying toward the flag, set in the right half of the green. I carefully go through my preshot routine, shifting my weight till it feels balanced. I draw the club back slowly, rhythmically. I see my left shoulder come under my chin, signifying a full, strong turn. I fire the right side.

And I yank the ball into the woods.

I don't know why that happened. I follow precisely the same routine with a provisional ball a few minutes later and hit the provisional ball onto the green. That's golf. It's a mental game. You not only have to know how to hit the shot. You have to be able to hit it when it counts. I didn't.

The Bug and the Rocket, meanwhile, hit their first tee shots onto the green and look likely to make par.

I find my ball eventually, lying on a patch of sand so deep in the woods that it seems likely that the alligators would be afraid to go back there. I have some nasty vegetation between myself and the green, so I declare the first ball unplayable. I two-putt with the provisional ball, add the stroke-and-distance penalty, put five on the scorecard, and figure that the

Groundhog Cup is out of reach unless something unlikely happens.

All three of us drive it into the fairway on No. 18, an uphill par four to a severely undulating green. I am short, so I hit first. It's a good shot, a pressure-free shot, clearing the front bunkers and rolling up somewhere near the hole. The Rocket hits a weak fade toward the green, leaving himself short and right.

Now it's the Bug's turn. A par will win it for him. So, most likely, will a bogey. The Bug is showing his normal sign of nervousness, chewing on a towel.

The Bug yanks it to the edge of a parking lot thirty yards left of the green.

"Getting ugly out here," L.T. observes. "Don't any of you guys want to win?"

The Bug follows the example I set on the previous hole, hitting a provisional into the fringe just short of the green. When he eventually finds his ball, it's sitting under an acacia bush about a foot from the bumper of someone's gray Cadillac. He elects to declare it unplayable and play the provisional, as I did, with the stroke-and-distance penalty.

By now readers familiar with Rule 27-2 (c) of the Rules of Golf are probably wondering what network televised the Groundhog Cup so they can call in and report a violation. I erred about the rules, and Bug erred in thinking I knew the rules. The rule is that you can declare a ball lost and play a provisional ball with a stroke-and-distance penalty. Or you can find a ball, declare it unplayable, and go back and play another ball from the same spot with a stroke-and-distance penalty. But you can't hit a bad shot, hit a provisional, find the original, and decide you're better off taking the penalty and playing the provisional. That is deemed playing a wrong ball. The rules provide that a player who plays a wrong ball and fails to correct the mistake immediately is disqualified.

Which the Bug and I are, after a prolonged discussion is finally resolved by the resident rules authority in the Copperhead pro shop. The Rocket, who kept his head when all around him were losing theirs, wins the Groundhog Cup, the original purse, and the Calcutta. Kelso and Barnyard slip in for place and show money.

"If that's the rule, what the hell," the Bug shrugs. "I had a good time anyway."

So did I, I finally decide after a couple of hours spent numbly staring at the Super Bowl preview show back in the condo, thinking about that bad swing on the seventeenth tee, thinking about the pain of disqualification, feeling particularly lousy because I misled the Bug. I come to this conclusion when I reflect on the way I felt back on that penultimate tee, just before I hit my disastrous shot. Playing with these guys had helped me experience a moment of intense and complete engagement on that tee, a moment such as life affords all too rarely. That, I decide, is what the camaraderie of the game is all about. We help one another reach such moments.

There remains only the bittersweet van ride through the twilight back to the Tampa airport. Everyone is fatigued, finally golfed out. There's a little talk about the upcoming Super Bowl. There's a little talk about whether to come back to Innisbrook for next year's Groundhog Cup or try another resort. We reach the airport, check our bags, and look for someplace to eat and watch the first quarter of the Super Bowl before our plane departs. We find a cafeteria on the shopping concourse.

I look around. The Rocket is nowhere in sight. Quickly, surreptitiously, I buy, peel, and eat a banana.

Mulligan Boys

Golf is a game in which attitude of mind accounts for incomparably more than mightiness of muscle.

—Haultain

In central Florida in mid-July, the supply of golf temporarily outstrips the demand for it. With temperatures in the nineties and winter tourists gone, courses that command a hundred dollars for a round in midwinter place little ads in the back pages of the sports section of the local papers, nestled amid pitches for investment advice, halitosis treatment, and impotence therapy. Come and play our course for only $29.95, one says. Try us for only $22, says another, and we'll throw in a free sleeve of balls. Offer good through September 30.

This is the high season of the Mulligan Boys.

Mulligan Boys are men engaged in the midlife equivalent of running away and joining the circus. They are in their late forties or early fifties. They have quit their jobs and sold their homes and moved to Florida to play professional golf in mini-tour leagues with names like the Forty-Plus Tour of Florida, leagues that use the semivacant courses of summertime Florida. They are honing their games for a crack at the Senior PGA Tour.

They offer yet another answer to the question of why people play golf. When they get to a certain age, it's because they still can.

A few years ago the editors of *Golf* magazine sent me down to Orlando to write an article about these rookies with graying hair and extravagant dreams. I arranged to link up with the senior division of an entry-level pro circuit called the Tommy Armour Tour at the Mission Inn in Howey-in-the-Hills, Florida.

"You might want to have a look at David Oakley," the tour's director and organizer, a cheerful man named Terry Fine, told me over the telephone. "He's been winning about sixty percent of our senior events."

When I arrived at the Mission Inn, I found none of the trappings associated with professional golf on the level of the PGA Tour. There were no ticket sellers, no orange-vested attendants directing me to park in a pasture a half mile from the course. There were no corporate tents, no grandstands. There was just a somnolent, off-season hotel with two golf courses. The Tommy Armour Tour had set up shop on a folding table by the El Campeon course's scoreboard. Its event that week had two divisions, one open and one for seniors. The open division tended to draw kids just out of college who were aiming for the PGA Tour or the Nike Tour. The senior event had attracted a field of three—Charlie Walters, Dana Messer, and Oakley.

"Take a cart," Terry Fine said. "They should be out around the fourth by now."

It was hot enough that I was grateful for the offer of transportation. I set off. The tournament was being held on the newer of the Mission Inn's two courses, Las Colinas. Like a lot of new Florida courses, it had an open, sun-baked appearance. No doubt the land had been producing oranges not too many years before. I passed a few groups of young men and slowed down long enough to watch them hitting irons to a green that looked to be a full furlong away. Except for the Tommy Armour Tour players, the course seemed to be deserted.

I found the senior division field on the fifth hole, a par five of four hundred and sixty-three yards from the white tees, which they were playing. At first glance they could have been any threesome of middle-aged men, riding in carts, perhaps sneaking in a round while the wife trundled the grandchildren around Disney World. One of them wielded a Killer Bee driver with a shaft the length of a flagstick. Another had a swing that looked like a beach chair unfolding. His backswing had three distinct segments.

And then there was Oakley. He was slender, with an easy rhythm to his swing. He had iron-colored hair, lightly tanned skin that lacked the distressed-leather look of most middle-aged golf pros, and thin, fine features that in a Jane Austen novel might have been described as refined. With his long, delicate fingers he could have passed for a musician, perhaps a flutist, on holiday from a symphony orchestra. He hit a high, controlled draw.

I watched the players hit their tee shots. Oakley turned to me. "Can we help you?" he asked pleasantly.

I introduced myself, told them why I was there.

Oakley smiled. "Great. Glad to have you."

I tagged along for the rest of the round, chatting occasionally with all three players. Walters was having a difficult time getting used to his long driver. Once in a while he'd find the right tempo for it and pop the ball down the fairway two-hundred and seventy-five yards. But just as often, he'd hit a low hook into a marsh. He finished his round at around 80.

Messer was just plain having difficulties; at the end of the round, he didn't even hand in a card. He was a short, round-bellied man with a gap-toothed smile and a red-white-and-blue Ben Hogan Co. golf bag. His name was printed on a piece of white cardboard slipped into a plastic sleeve on the bag.

That, he explained to me between the fourteenth and fifteenth holes, was because he sometimes resorted to hustling tourists during the winter. He couldn't convince his marks he had a twelve handicap if he had a professional's bag with the name stitched into it. But a professional likes to have a bag with his name on it. The plastic sleeve and the cardboard sign were Messer's compromise. When he took the card out, his ungainly swing made it easy to get games with pigeons, guys just off the plane from Chicago or New York with expensive clubs and creaky swings. Then he'd stick the name card back in the plastic sleeve and spend his winnings on entry fees for events on circuits like the Tommy Armour Tour. Messer had an array of trick shots developed during a life misspent on a lot of golf courses. He could, for instance, stand in a fairway with his back to the flag and, without turning around, hit a ball on the green from one hundred and fifty yards. He'd won some money betting people he could do that, he told me proudly.

But he didn't, on this day at least, have the game to come close to David Oakley. Oakley made a couple of stylish birdies on the back nine to finish with a 70. With half the Senior Division tournament done and a ten-stroke lead, he was a cinch to rack up another Tommy Armour Tour win. Of course, that would barely earn him enough money to keep himself in golf balls.

On minor league circuits like the Tommy Armour Tour, players basically provide the prize money with their entry fees. It might cost $250 to play a thirty-six-hole event. The tour organizer keeps a cut of the pooled entry fees for administrative expenses. Another slice goes to the golf course owner. The players split what is left. Depending on the size of the field, first prize might be anywhere from $500 to $2,500. A player who consistently finishes first or second might eke out a living on such a circuit. The rest are, in effect, paying for playing lessons, for a chance to learn what it feels like to play golf for prize money, with every stroke counted.

Oakley graciously accepted when I told him that *Golf* would be happy to pick up the tab for lunch after his round. We went to the grill off the Mission Inn locker room. He ordered a sandwich and a beer. He sprinkled salt in the beer before he drank any.

I knew a little bit about Oakley already. Up until a year prior to our meeting, he'd been managing a discount furniture store in Woodbridge, Virginia. He'd been playing amateur golf in the Washington area, winning a lot of club tournaments but nothing on the national level. One summer's day shortly after his forty-ninth birthday, he'd walked into his boss's office and quit. He'd turned pro, sold his house, and moved to Orlando to get ready for a crack at the Senior Tour. As we ate, he told me more about himself.

For a first-class player, Oakley got a late start. Neither of his parents were especially keen golfers, but when he was fifteen, they joined a club in the Virginia suburbs of Washington, primarily for the swimming facilities. Oakley took quickly and easily to golf. He played two years on the varsity at Falls Church High School. He finished tied for second in the Virginia state high school championships.

But golfers are like violinists. The best of them, the prodigies, have been playing for years by the time they're fifteen, winning national junior championships. Oakley's high school golf exploits attracted no college interest. He went to the University of Florida without an athletic scholarship.

Florida had some excellent golfers in those years. Bob Murphy, an NCAA individual champion and a future Tour star, led the team in Oakley's junior year. Steve Melnyk, a U.S. Amateur champion, was the top player in Oakley's senior year. Oakley tried out for the Florida team, made it, and was a contributor. He won a couple of events, but he was not the star. Murphy and Melnyk, he recalled, "were a big cut above me."

When Oakley finished college, the Vietnam War was at its peak. Rather than risk being drafted, he joined the U.S. Public Health Service for two years, working as a statistician. He played as much golf as he could. When he won the Mid-Atlantic Amateur in 1969, he decided to give professional golf a shot.

He entered the Tour's qualifying school, a two-tier tournament that is among the more arduous rites of passage in sport. There is no schooling involved in qualifying school, except in the sense that playing golf under extreme pressure is a learning experience. Qualifying school is an elongated tournament to determine which golfers earn playing privileges on a given tour for the following year. Oakley got to the second stage of the 1970 qualifying school but missed the qualifying number by five strokes. He bounced around minor professional circuits in Florida, Canada, and Asia for a while, then tried qualifying school again in 1971. Again he reached the second stage. He went to Palm Beach, where the low twenty-three scores and ties over six rounds would earn the right to enter PGA Tour events. Among those in the field were Lanny Wadkins and David Graham. Oakley shot 445. A score of 444 won a card. (In fact, 445 should have been good enough. But a pro from South America falsified his scorecard and gave himself 444. He was kicked off the Tour when the cheating was discovered, but by then the Tour decided it was too late to go back and recalculate the results.)

Oakley kept at it for another year. He missed winning the Thailand Open by a shot. He finished a shot back in the Spanish Open. Then he failed to get past the first cut in the 1972 qualifying school. He had a wife and a two-year-old son. What he didn't have, he decided, was something internal, a killer instinct that separated players like Murphy and Graham and Wadkins from players like him. He quit professional golf.

He worked as a hotel liquidator for a number of years, buying and reselling furnishings from hotels that were bankrupt or remodeling. He got divorced. He got his amateur status back. He worked as a store manager for a furniture retailer. He remarried, bought a house in the suburbs, and had another child. He played golf when he could squeeze out time for it, in between the store's big sales days. He won five club championships and lost in the finals four times.

And he started seeing a new sports phenomenon on television, the Senior PGA Tour. It was the growth sport of the 1980s, fueled by the public's continuing desire to see the likes of Snead and Palmer, Player and Trevino. By the time Oakley entered his late forties, his old college teammate, Murphy, was enjoying a second career on the Senior Tour, making several million dollars at it. Friends started telling Oakley he was good enough to get a piece of that money and that glory for himself. Oakley started to listen to them. He waited until he got a semiannual bonus in June. Once the check cleared, he gave his notice.

His boss, he recalled, was happy for him. Most people are when they encounter a Mulligan Boy. They wish him luck. They hope it works out. Oakley stayed on long enough to train his replacement, then left the furniture store and turned pro again.

His luck was not good. Within a few months a blood test indicated he had cancer of the prostate. He had surgery to remove it. The surgery and postoperative treatment were deemed successful. But Oakley lost weight. He lost practice time. He was uninsured, so he lost a chunk of the money he'd been counting on to see him through his quest to qualify for the Senior Tour. He played the U.S. Senior Open that year wearing a diaper because the surgery had temporarily made him incontinent.

But Oakley had two important things going for him. One was a naturally buoyant, resilient personality. He was the sort of man who refused to dwell on setbacks, choosing instead to focus on the opportunities that lay before him. Over the months to come, I would speak to him several times after he failed in one competition or another. He never sounded discouraged. "I'm loving life," he would say.

His other big advantage was his wife, Doris. She was the sort of woman who, faced with a choice between a happy husband and a husband with a growing IRA, instinctively chose happy. When she wasn't looking after their son, Chris, she followed Oakley through important tournament rounds, swapping ideas with other golf spouses for sandwiches that would keep a player's energy level up through a difficult back nine.

The odds against Oakley succeeding in his endeavor were high. From its inception the Senior Tour had been less about competition than the regular Tour and more about nostalgia. This was understandable. Its players couldn't be marketed as the best in the world. But they could be sold as the best liked. The rules were set up to make it as probable as possible that fans paying for tickets or watching a broadcast would get to see familiar faces—Palmer and Player, Nicklaus and Trevino, Rodriguez and Floyd. There was no cut after thirty-six holes on the Senior Tour, so any big name who entered a tournament would be around for the weekend. The eligibility rules for the Senior Tour were set up to favor players with long and winning records on the regular Tour.

There was room in the mix for players who had never made it on the regular Tour, for people like Tom Wargo, who used to operate a driving range in Illinois. But not for a lot of them. An occasional Wargo victory made for a nice human interest story. A succession of tournaments won by former club pros and driving range operators made for low television ratings and diminishing space in the newspapers. So the rules provided that only eight players could make it each year through the Senior Tour qualifying school. Once on the Senior Tour, such players had to make the top thirty-one on the money list to remain eligible for the following year's events. Otherwise, it was back to school.

Oakley was undaunted. He outlined for me his strategy. He

was going to play the Tommy Armour Tour and the Forty-Plus Tour in Florida for a while. He'd also enter some Senior Series events; the Senior Series was a circuit that aspired to be to senior golf what the Nike Tour was to the PGA Tour or what Triple-A baseball was to the major leagues. There were senior events in Europe that he might qualify for. Then in November he'd have the tournament that really mattered, the Senior Tour qualifying school.

He felt that he had the game to succeed. "If you shoot even par for eight rounds, you will usually finish in the top eight at the qualifying school," he said. "If you can average one under par per round on the Senior Tour, you can make a lot of money."

That was true, and that was part of the lure of senior golf. There were lots of middle-aged men in America with handicaps of scratch or better who looked at those numbers and saw themselves teeing it up with Nicklaus and Floyd, saw themselves as the next Wargo or Larry Laoretti (former club pros who had won the PGA Seniors and the U.S. Senior Open, respectively). They knew they could hit it as far and putt as well as those players. They knew they could shoot par or better.

After a week in Florida watching Oakley and other aspiring Senior Tour players, though, I started to see some differences between them and the successful seniors I saw on television. They were subtle but important. The successful seniors almost always gave themselves a makeable birdie putt when they had a short iron to a green, usually one of ten feet or less. The wannabes might hit their drives as far, but their wedges were not as sharp. Their birdie putts were from twenty feet instead of ten, and so they made fewer of them. The elite seniors also knew how to manage their games. If they hit a fairway bunker off the tee on a par five, they first made certain they got out of the trap, then tried to make a birdie with a good approach and a good putt. The wannabe, in the same bunker, might take a wood and go for the green. He might hit the lip and wind up with a six.

Oakley had seen other differences. He thought chipping and putting were factors that separated successful seniors from wannabes. So he practiced chipping and putting every day. He'd taken a lesson at the David Leadbetter Golf Academy in Orlando aimed at giving him greater distance with his long irons. He felt he was improving in each of those aspects.

One thing was certain. He never, he said, felt any urge to go back to work in a furniture store.

I kept in touch occasionally with Oakley over the next year and a half. He made it to the second stage of qualifying school in his first attempt, then missed the top eight by a half-dozen strokes. "That's all right," he told me over the phone. "I feel like I accomplished a lot just getting that far."

He went to Europe in his second summer as a pro and had a great campaign. He was in the final group in the final round of the Senior British Open, playing against Bob Charles, a former British Open champion, and Brian Barnes, a former British Ryder Cup team member. He finished tied for second with Charles, but he acquitted himself well. "That convinced me I could play with the big boys," he told me afterward.

In the fall of 1996, Oakley entered the qualifying school yet again. This time he shot a steady 71-70-71-71 during the second stage at the TPC at Sawgrass. He birdied the final hole to finish fourth and secure his card. He danced around the green and bear-hugged his caddie. Thirty years after graduating from college, Oakley had finally made it to a major professional circuit.

Of course, I followed his progress as closely as I could during the 1997 season. He started out a little hesitantly, shooting 75-76-74 in the Royal Caribbean Classic down in Florida, finishing tied for sixtieth and earning $1,488. Over the next month he seemed to be slowly getting acclimated, finishing fifty-second, thirty-third, and forty-third. Then, in the Toshiba Senior Classic, he shot 69, 71, and 72 to tie for twentieth and earn $11,171. I thought that he had hit his stride.

But he hadn't. He followed that up with some mediocre tournaments, then a fairly strong one, then a few mediocre ones. It might not have been a bad start for a rookie, except for the pressure he was under to make the top thirty-one on the season's money list. A tournament in which he finished at two under par and earned $8,580, as he did in the Bell South Classic at Opryland, was not a success because he finished tied for thirty-third. At that pace he wouldn't make the end-of-the-year cut. He would have to face the long odds of qualifying school again.

By autumn, when I finally got a chance to see him play, it was evident that only a stretch of brilliant golf could move Oakley into the top thirty-one. He'd won about $130,000. He was sixty-fifth on the money list. He had five events left when I caught up with him in Winston-Salem, North Carolina, at the Vantage Classic. He was on the practice tee, hitting wedges.

If Oakley felt pressured, he did not show it. He greeted me with exactly the same mixture of politeness and warmth I'd encountered back at the Mission Inn. His kit showed a few changes. He had a couple of manufacturers' logos on his bag and his hat, a sign of the sort of small endorsement deals that come to virtually anyone who earns a card on the PGA Tour or the Senior Tour. He had a Florida Gator headcover on his driver and "The Oak" stitched into his bag. But he still looked delicate. He still hit a sweet, controlled draw.

He finished with his wedges and we walked over to the putting green. He rolled putts for half an hour, then told me his workday was over. He was not playing in the pro-am event that afternoon, so he'd be going back to his motel to rest.

Playing or not playing in the pro-am is one of the ways in which class is distinguished and hierarchy is established on the Senior Tour. There are perhaps thirty-six slots available in the pro-am events, which generally combine one professional with four amateurs, each of whom pays several thousand dollars for the privilege of playing. Most professionals like playing in pro-ams, if for no other reason than that it's the only way to get a practice round in on the day before the tournament. Tournament directors thus can and do choose the elite players to fill their pro-am fields. Players like Oakley can stay on the practice range or go back to their rooms.

There were other class distinctions, Oakley said. Players in his category generally teed off very early in the morning or very late in the afternoon. They either had dewy greens or chewed up greens to contend with. They might or might not get courtesy cars. They were never paired in the early rounds with famous players or tournament winners. These distinctions, Oakley said, weren't anything to complain about. They were just reminders that even though he had his Senior Tour card, he hadn't quite arrived.

I hung around the practice tee after Oakley left, watching Hale Irwin hit iron shots. Irwin was the dominant figure on the Senior Tour that season, and it was not hard to understand why. He was striking the ball superbly, aiming at a flag about a hundred and fifty yards from the practice tee. One shot after another landed within ten feet of the flag. Using perhaps a seven-iron, he hit his shots closer to his target than Oakley had hit his wedges to his target when I watched him earlier. Irwin might not have had the length any longer to compete with the very best players in the world. But I found it hard to imagine that there were many players, of whatever age and on whatever tour, who could match him from one hundred and fifty yards in.

I couldn't stay to watch Irwin move down to his longer clubs, though, because there was someone else I wanted to see. Arnold Palmer was playing in the pro-am. By my calculations his group ought soon to be arriving at the eighth hole, adjacent to the practice range. I moved over there.

Palmer's presence was heralded a few moments later by a thickening of the gallery around the eighth, which was a two-hundred-and-eight-yard par three. It wasn't a crowd really. Senior Tour events don't draw crowds on pro-am days. But the few dozen spectators around the green became a few hundred as they were joined by the winter soldiers of Arnie's Army.

Then a golf ball came flying down from the tee. It landed in the clipped grass a few yards short of the green, hopped in the air, then rolled to the back fringe, maybe thirty feet from the hole. I looked down toward the tee. I could make out a figure in a bright magenta golf shirt and gray slacks. He had white hair. It was Palmer.

I confess that my eyes got a little moist when I recognized him. Arnold Palmer was one of the heroes of my boyhood. I could remember watching him win his first Masters in 1958 on a little black-and-white television set; he threw his visor to the crowd around the final green. By 1960, his best year, my whole family would gather to watch a golf telecast if Palmer was in contention. Even my mother, who didn't know a seven-iron from a Seven-Eleven store, would yell, "Charge!" when he started sinking putts and lashing drives and making birdies. I could remember as well watching in consternation when he lost playoffs at the Open in 1962 and 1963 and, most painfully, 1966. Though I had never so much as shaken his hand, I felt as if Palmer and I had been through a lot together, through moments of bold, exhilarating triumph and crushing defeat.

I had, of course, had other heroes in other sports. I liked Willie Mays in baseball, Frank Gifford in football, and John Thomas in the high jump. They had faded away. My last memories of them were often sad ones: Mays trying and failing to get around on mediocre fastballs during his misbegotten stint with the Mets in 1972; Gifford lying motionless on the field, leveled by Eagles linebacker Chuck Bednarik; Thomas trying and failing to beat the Soviet jumper Valery

Brumel, who seemed to have his number. Age was not kind to them.

But Palmer, as he aged, continued to provide moments to enjoy and admire. Occasionally it was a flash of the old brilliance—a triumph in the U.S. Senior Open or the holes-in-one he made on consecutive days at the TPC at Avenel when that course opened back in 1987. More often, though, it was the way he handled himself. I remembered seeing Palmer during a practice round prior to the PGA Championship at Inverness in 1993. Between holes an elderly couple ducked under the ropes and approached him. The woman carried a little Kodak box camera; the man had a hopeful look on his face. Without hesitating, Palmer draped an arm around the man's shoulder, smiled, and posed for a picture. I liked that. I liked the way he took a paternal interest in young Tiger Woods, playing practice rounds with him at Augusta. I liked the quiet and dignified way he had coped with prostate cancer.

Palmer stood at the edge of the white tee box while his amateur partners hit their shots, then strode down the fairway with the same erect head, the same little swagger that I remembered. His face didn't have the fierce concentration of the Palmer in my mind's eye; nor, thankfully, did the real Palmer have the cigarette cupped in his hands that I remembered from the '60s, a cigarette that he smoked with the dashing demeanor of a silent movie hero preparing to face, defiantly, a firing squad. He was involved with the gallery more than I remembered him, nodding and smiling to acknowledge its applause.

He waited until it was his turn to play, then hunched over his putt, peeking at the hole. The stroke, when it came, was a jabby one. I hoped for a moment that the ball would go in, but it had no chance. He was two feet wide of the mark and tapped in for a routine par. A groan from the gallery. More applause.

I followed him to the ninth tee. Palmer hit a good drive, maybe two hundred and fifty yards down the fairway. Then he watched the amateurs hit from the white tees. One of them managed to push a ball out past his, and Palmer clapped him on the back. He had some teasing words for one of the other members of the foursome, some banter with one of the wives following the group. He seemed to be enjoying himself immensely.

For some reason this surprised me. I had been assuming that Palmer's presence at the Vantage Classic was connected in some way to the fact that Wake Forest University, his alma mater, is also located in Winston-Salem. Why else, I had thought, would a man of sixty-eight, a man just eight months past cancer surgery, a man with more money than he could ever spend, bother to leave home and play in a meaningless Senior Tour event? The likelihood, I figured, was that the costs of operating his plane would be more than the prize money Palmer would win.

Perhaps there was some connection to Wake Forest behind Palmer's appearance, but it struck me that that was not the primary reason. Palmer was playing the Vantage Classic because he wanted to, because he liked it. He delighted in the fact that he could play the game. Maybe a younger Palmer would have hit a different kind of tee shot to the eighth green, a higher shot that landed near the pin, bit, and stopped instead of a low shot that chased on. Maybe a younger Palmer would have stroked the birdie putt a lot more smoothly, maybe even holed it. But the salient fact was that Palmer could still put the ball on the green, could still make par. I suspect that somewhere in the back of his mind, Palmer entertained the thought that maybe if his putter got hot he could still contend, perhaps still win.

I hoped he would.

I met David Oakley for dinner that night at a place called the Macaroni Grill, across a shopping mall parking lot from the Hampton Inn, where he was staying. It was one of those chain Italian eateries that you find nowadays in similar shopping malls near similar Interstate highway exit ramps all across the country. Local American cuisine, I'm afraid, is going the way of local American accents in a homogenized society.

Gil Morgan, the hot new player in the senior ranks at the time, walked into the restaurant at the same time we did. He and Oakley said hello pleasantly, but Morgan didn't suggest that we dine together. Nor did Oakley. That pecking order again.

Oakley said he normally ate with his true peers on the Senior Tour, the ones, like him, who had never played the regular Tour and had yet to win on the Senior Tour. The major exception he could remember had occurred at the Senior Players Championship in Michigan, which threw a banquet for the players on the eve of the competition.

The tournament was special enough that Doris Oakley flew up from Florida to watch it. Somehow or other, Doris met Barbara Nicklaus during an activity arranged for the players' spouses. Barbara Nicklaus, who has a reputation for being gracious, had taken Doris Oakley under her wing. When the Oakleys arrived for the banquet that night, dressed up and feeling a little nervous, Barbara had smiled and said to Doris, "Come sit with us." So the Oakleys dined that night with the Nicklauses, the Stocktons, and the Floyds.

"A photographer came and took a picture of the group," Oakley said. "It's not hard to identify Doris and me. We're the ones grinning so hard our faces are about to come apart."

We poured some Chianti and ordered pasta.

Oakley had actually played a round with Nicklaus, he recalled, but it was a matter of happenstance. He was at The Tradition, a major event for the seniors held at a Nicklaus-designed course in Arizona. Oakley was about to start a practice round when Jim Albus walked up and asked to come along. Albus has won some senior events, but he and Oakley had been friends since they were both scrambling to make some money on the Asian Tour in the early 1970s. Oakley was glad to have his company.

Before they could hit their drives, Nicklaus walked up and asked Albus, whom he knew, if he could play with them.

"Fine with me, Jack. All right with you, Dave?" Albus asked.

Oakley swallowed. "Sure," he said.

Albus introduced them. Oakley managed not to say how long he had admired and revered Nicklaus. And he managed to keep his golf ball out of the desert for the first few holes. Then they came to the fifth, a par five of the sort that critics of Nicklaus-the-architect have contended he designs to suit his own game. It was well over five hundred yards long, and the green was separated from the fairway by a "transition area," a strip of untouched desert sand and rock. The green was reachable in two by a player who could hit a long drive and then a high, accurate fade with a long iron—the sorts of shots that Nicklaus, in his prime, hit better than anyone.

A fairly stiff wind was favoring the players, and Oakley drove the ball well, though not as far as Nicklaus and Albus. He was the first to hit his second shot. He was maybe two hundred and fifty yards away, and he hit a three-wood. The ball landed at the end of the fairway and bounced through the transition area, which was dry and hard. It rolled up onto the green.

Nicklaus turned around and looked at Oakley. "I didn't think anyone could do that," he said. The implication in his voice was that no one was supposed to be able to do that.

Oakley had shrugged, not displeased with himself. He smiled as he told me the story, savoring the moment yet again.

Oakley hit another shot through a transition area to reach the eighteenth green. As he walked down that fairway, he saw Nicklaus talking to a member of the course maintenance crew. Before he left the course that evening, he saw crew members out in the transition area in front of the eighteenth green, adding sand and gravel to soften it up and make sure no one would be able to run a ball through it during the tournament. Jack Nicklaus did not want the likes of David Oakley making birdies on his par fives, at least not that way.

That was about Oakley's only brush with the greats of the game. Of course, he pointed out, there was an obvious way for him to move up in the senior hierarchy. He could start shooting lower scores. In the final rounds of an event, the pairings and starting times are determined on the basis of the standings. The leaders play with one another and get the last tee times. If Oakley wanted a chance to play more often with the Irwins, the Morgans, and the Nicklauses, the door was open. All he had to do to go through it was start shooting some 67s and 66s in the early rounds.

The next day I went back out to the golf course to see if Oakley could start doing that. He was in a threesome with Bobby Stroble and Will Sowles. Like Oakley, they had no credentials from the regular PGA Tour. Sowles was a Tennesseean who'd played a couple of times in the U.S. Amateur before he turned pro in 1996 and finished second at the Senior Tour qualifying school. Stroble, a thick-bodied black man, had learned to play golf in the army. He'd knocked around as a pro for nearly thirty years before he finally made it to the Senior Tour in 1995. He'd managed to make the top thirty-one in 1996 to retain his card, but he'd not yet won a tournament.

Half-a-dozen people followed this threesome as they played. They were in the tournament, but there was a sense that they weren't really of it. The tournament, as far as most of the spectators and the corporate sponsors were concerned, was where Irwin and Palmer and Morgan were playing.

When Oakley, Stroble, and Sowles played a hole, it seemed as if all the marshals and scoreboards and gallery ropes weren't necessary, that they were waiting for someone else.

Oakley was hitting the ball fairly well, putting his tee shots in the fairways, hitting them a little longer than I remembered from his days in Florida on the Tommy Armour Tour. But he made a few mistakes with his scoring clubs, his wedge and his putter. At this level such mistakes were fatal. On the second hole, a short par four, he drove to about eighty yards from the green. But he got his wedge no closer than twenty feet and then left his birdie putt six inches short. On the sixth, a par five, he set himself up at the right distance for a wedge third into the green. But he hit it fat and missed the green. He chipped to four feet, then missed the par putt. Bogey.

By the end of the round, he was three over par, with a 74. He was eight strokes off the pace set by Irwin, and his slim chance of moving into the top thirty-one spots on the money list had gotten appreciably slimmer.

And, in fact, David Oakley did not keep his card after the 1997 season. Nor did he make it through qualifying school for the 1998 or 1999 seasons. Instead, he filled his schedule with events on Florida circuits like the Tommy Armour Tour, with Senior Series events, with European events. It was not the sort of decade that Merrill Lynch would recommend for a man in his fifties, not the sort of probity that leads to the secure, early retirement the investment firms tell us we should be planning for in the commercials they run during golf telecasts.

On the other hand, there was no end of fiftyish men going to offices every day in jobs they disliked, telling themselves that if they could stick it out for ten more years, they could move to Florida and play as much golf as they liked.

Which was what David Oakley was doing.

A couple of years later, when he was fifty-four, I heard good news about Oakley. He'd broken through in a way, winning an event on the European Seniors Tour called the MDIS & Partners Festival of Golf at Ascot, England. He'd done well in several other European seniors events that spring, winning a total of about $30,000 in prize money and earning a three-year exemption from qualifying for senior tournaments over there. If it was not quite the equivalent, in prestige or prize money, of winning on the Senior Tour in the United States, it was nonetheless a sign of progress.

I caught up with Oakley shortly after he returned from that sojourn in Europe. He was playing in a qualifying round for the U.S. Senior Open on a drizzly June Monday at Wood-more Country Club in Mitchellville, Maryland. It was the kind of round that a player in Oakley's category becomes familiar with. From a field of about forty players, two would qualify for the tournament proper, which would be held in Des Moines two weeks hence. Prevailing would earn Oakley nothing except the chance to move on. Failing would mean a wasted drive up to Maryland from Florida and a long ride home with his thoughts. He had, in short, nothing to gain and a lot to lose.

Oakley was on the ninth hole when I found his group, and he hit a beautiful shot into the green, a ball that checked up on the safe side of the flag, caught a slope in the terrain, and trickled slowly down to within five feet of the hole. But then he was too careful with the putt, and he made only a par.

He didn't seem bothered by it, though, when he saw me standing by the tenth tee. He shook hands, told me he thought I'd lost some weight. I said he was swinging well.

"Yeah, I am," he said. "Hitting the ball well."

He was one under par at that point. He thought it would take a final score of three under par to be certain of getting one of the two qualifying spots.

I walked with Oakley along the back nine at Woodmore, a tough new course cut through a wooded wetland with a lot of humps and swales built into the greens. He was playing nearly immaculate golf, driving his ball into the fairways, hitting the greens. He got one of the birdies he thought he'd need on the tenth hole, sinking a twenty-foot putt.

Knowing what was at stake, I agonized through Oakley's round. On the eleventh and fourteenth holes, he left himself five-foot par putts. He managed to roll them in. On the fifteenth he set himself up for a birdie with a nice wedge to about seven feet. But the putt slid by the hole. "Goddam it," Oakley muttered, slapping his thigh in frustration.

I decided that, while quitting one's job at the age of fifty and becoming a golf pro was a pleasant fantasy, the reality was quite a bit less pleasant. The reality was that if you did what David Oakley had done, your standard of living and your self-esteem could become dependent on whether a handful of five-foot putts dropped in or slid by the hole. I didn't want to put that kind of pressure on my golf game. But I admired Oakley for being willing to try it.

Though he wanted another birdie badly, Oakley had the sense not to be reckless. He parred the long sixteenth after hitting a fine drive and a precise five-wood to the middle of the green. He caught a bad break on the seventeenth, driving in the fairway but finding his approach to the green blocked by trees. He managed to chip up and sink another five-footer to save his par. And on the final hole, a par five, he took an iron for his second shot, laying up rather than trying a two-hundred-thirty-yard approach to an elevated green guarded by water. He thought he could hit a wedge into the green with his third shot and stop it near the pin. But the wedge landed twenty-five feet past the pin and for some reason refused to spin back. Oakley made his par and posted his score, a 70.

"That's the low score so far," the USGA man told Oakley.

"The guys I'm worried about are still out on the course," Oakley replied.

He didn't do what I might have done, which was to hang around the scorer's table or commandeer a cart and go back onto the course to see how his rivals were faring. He went into the clubhouse to have lunch. There could be, he knew, a playoff after everyone was finished. He didn't want to be famished if there was.

As we ate, he told me more about his European success. He'd missed the cut in his first event, in Turkey, but he attributed that to jet lag. The next week, in Ireland, he closed with a 67 to finish eleventh. The week after that, he'd been paired for the final round with Tommy Horton, the leading money winner among the European seniors. "Everyone expected me to fold," he recalled with satisfaction. "But I shot a 69 and won by six strokes."

In fact, his average for the four final rounds he'd played in Europe was a shade under 69. He was, he thought, learning how to play his best golf under pressure.

A group of Woodmore members came into the room, quietly jubilant. Their head pro, Larry Ringer, had finished with a 68. Oakley now stood a precarious second. If anyone out on the course came in with a 69, he was a loser.

I asked Oakley how he was holding up financially, if he'd ever come close to scraping bottom.

"This past winter was pretty rough," he said. "It used to be I could make two or three thousand a month playing mini-tour events. But this winter, for some reason, the senior events were not full. You'd enter for a hundred dollars, win, and your check would be a hundred and fifteen dollars. It was a good thing I won some money in Europe."

He did not, though, spend much time wondering whether his life would be more secure if he hadn't chosen to pursue golf. For one thing, the furniture store chain he'd worked for had recently declared bankruptcy. Even if he'd stayed on the conventional path in life, he might have had money worries.

More important, he had faith in himself and his golf game. He was still improving, still learning. The track records of most senior players show that their performance starts to fall off after the age of fifty-five. But he felt fit. He was working out. He didn't think that would happen to him. He thought, to the contrary, that if he kept knocking on the door, one of these days it would open.

We walked out into drizzle to check the scoreboard. All but one group was in. No one besides Ringer and Oakley had broken par. Then the final scores were posted—none under 75. Oakley was back in the Senior Open field. I wished him luck in the tournament.

As I drove home, I thought about Oakley and Palmer. Golf afforded both of them something denied athletes in other sports. Well past the age at which Willie Mays and Frank Gifford and John Thomas had to quit, Palmer and Oakley were still in the arena, still striving, despite age, despite cancer. Oakley, indeed, was a rookie.

I have read commentaries by writers who dislike this aspect of the game. They say that golf can't be called a sport because middle-aged men can play it. They write that it's somehow sad or repugnant to see Palmer enter a tournament and shoot 76 or 79. They advise him to quit tournament play.

I think they've missed the point about golf. One of its finer attributes is precisely the fact that you don't have to be young to play it. Time works very slowly in eroding golfers' skills. A player who takes reasonable care of himself can hit the ball almost as far at fifty as he could at twenty. If he's observant as he plays, he can compensate for lost yardage with additional knowledge. A man in his forties can win the U.S. Open against the best young players in the world. David Oakley can be a better player at fifty-four than he was at fifty. Arnold Palmer, nearly seventy, can still tee it up at the Masters and the Bay Hill Invitational and make a few birdies.

That's not something to criticize or bemoan. It's something to celebrate.

Twilight Golf

*To sum up then, in what does the secret of golf lie? Not in one thing;
but in many.*

—Haultain

In my part of the world, twilight golf is a fleeting, seasonal
delicacy, like softshell crabs and fresh basil. Sometime in
early May the evenings get soft enough and long enough
that a golfer can finish dinner, drive to the course, and play
six, eight, or nine holes before dark. This possibility usually
lasts until early July, when the season of evening thunder-
storms arrives to curtail it. By August the diminution of the
sunlit hours again makes it impossible. But in May and June
there is no finer golf than twilight golf.

Partly, I think, it's the quality of the air on those late spring
and early summer evenings. The heat of the day has dissi-
pated, but the ground is still warm and the muscles loosen up
easily. A golfer sweats enough to feel comfortable at twilight,
but not enough to feel that an extra towel is needed. Sometimes, in the hollows of the course, the air is actually cool.

The quality of the light is special as well. It's no accident
that photographers who specialize in golf courses do all their

work just after the sun rises and just before it sets. In those hours the light is soft and luminous, and the grass looks its most plush. The trees cast long, graceful shadows. The effect on the course is like the effect of candlelight on the faces of the guests at a dinner party. The ordinary becomes handsome. The merely pretty becomes beautiful.

At twilight the game is stripped of its daytime formality. The starter is gone and the pro shop is closed. There are no starting times, no matches, no Nassaus, no scorecards. Those things have their place, I know. But I like the casualness of golf after dinner. I never open a fresh sleeve of balls at twilight; I play with the scuffed and dinged balls from the bottom of the bag pocket. If I'm wondering whether driver or three-wood is the right club off the tee on the first hole, I try both. If I don't like the way a shot comes off, I drop another ball and try again.

Playing a couple of balls doesn't matter because I'm not holding anyone up. The course is rarely really empty at twilight. It just feels that way. The other twilight golfers that I see don't strike me as competitors for space on the tee or people who are slowing me down. If I find myself behind a father with two small kids who are struggling to get the ball airborne, I just wave, silently wish the kids well, walk over to an open hole, and play it instead.

And there are fathers and kids around. Twilight is the ideal time to introduce kids to the game. There are no growling foursomes eager to finish their regular Saturday morning four-ball match before the football games start, wondering why kids are holding up the pace of play. There is just the golf course and the twilight. Paradoxically, there can seem to be more time, rather than less, when the sun is just about to go down.

Twilight is when I like to take my own kids to the course or, rather, when they agree to play with me. Neither my son nor my daughter plays a lot of golf. The boy has gravitated to sports like running and wrestling, in which he doesn't have to cope with a vexatious ball. He likes a simple contest pitting his strength and endurance against someone else's. The girl fell in love with horses when she was six years old.

They play a couple of formal rounds a year with me on family vacations. These are occasions when my uncle, who is seventy-five, gets the old family pictures down from the back of the hall closet and tells his nieces and nephews and great-nieces and great-nephews stories about the grandparents and great-grandparents they never knew. Noses in pictures are compared to noses on young faces. Resemblances are noted. Then everyone goes off for a round of golf. My uncle, who doesn't see too well anymore, takes a couple of the younger kids with him to help him find his golf balls and pull them out of the cup for him. The winner is usually someone who shoots 116 gross with a handicap of forty-eight strokes. They are precious times for me, and I can see myself, maybe, some-time in the future, being the one to pull the pictures out and have a child along to help me see my longer shots, such as they might be.

But sometimes after dinner on a summer evening, my kids come along for a few holes of twilight golf, just to humor the old man. The boy, in a mellow concession to convention, will pull a polo shirt on over his T-shirt. He likes to wear a yellow baseball hat with a green block "H" above the bill, a replica, he tells me, of the hats worn by the Hawaii Islanders of the old Pacific Coast League. The girl pulls her hair back in a ponytail and puts on something that doesn't smell too strongly of the stable. I root around in the garage for the old bags and old clubs. I hand them golf balls and tees. And off we go.

The last time this happened, the kids had trouble getting off the first tee. The boy blooped a shot off to the right, past the out-of-bounds stakes. The girl foozled her shot, dribbling it off the tee.

The boy jogged off to retrieve his ball from the edge of the practice range. The girl found hers in the rough in front of the tee. She pulled an iron from her bag, wound up, and hacked away. The ball moved just enough to give her the impression that it was mocking her effort—maybe a foot.

"Why can't I hit it?" she demanded.

She swung again, shanking the ball weakly off to the right. She watched it skitter away with all the impatient, annoyed disdain that a fourteen-year-old can muster.

"This is a stupid game," she said.

In my mind I composed a rebuttal. There was a man named Haultain, I would say. He wrote a book about golf you might find interesting. His thesis was that golf is a wonderful, fascinating game.

And why, she would reply, would anyone think that?

Haultain, I would say, decided that there was no single answer to that question. Golf fascinates us for a lot of reasons.

Like what, she might demand, a hand on her hip, her lower lip slightly curled.

Well, I would answer, there's the exploratory-assertive motivational system.

The what? She'd have a sneer in her voice by this time, a little disdain for the old man's creeping senility.

People get a charge out of bashing a ball, hitting it where they want it to go, I'd say.

Back on the real golf course, the girl hit a vicious push-slice that disappeared into the trees. I reached into my bag and tossed her another ball. She dropped it to the ground, eyed it with hostility.

"Why does it go off to the right like that?" she demanded.

I shrugged. "I've been trying to figure that out for a long time."

She glared some more at the new ball. To my mind it was innocent, but in hers it was marked by the original sin of all golf balls, disobedience.

Besides, I continued in my imaginary little seminar presentation, think about the golf course. Think about the clipped grass. Think about the places of prospect. Don't they resonate somewhere in your genes? Or do your genes seek a place of refuge? And look at the course itself. See the way the tree just in front of and to the right of the first green complicates the strategy of even this simple hole, makes it worth flirting with the trees and rough on the left side of the fairway in order to get a more open shot to the pin? Of all sporting venues, only a golf course offers that kind of interest and strategy.

I prefer the jumping course at a horse show, she'd grumble.

Back to reality. The girl topped a ball that at least stayed in the fairway and rolled fifty yards ahead. I picked up her bag and put it over my free shoulder. I saw her expression soften slightly. She has always liked the idea of Daddy as caddie.

The boy took a big hack at his ball and caught it cleanly. But he had suddenly too much club. The ball flew the green and disappeared in the rough beyond. Stoically, he picked up his bag and went after it. I walked beside the girl, wondering what else I could tell her.

There was always the Platonic ideal that floats beneath the surface of golf like a big, semighostly fish that swims beneath the surface of a river, manifesting itself in the shadows it casts and the ripples it makes. There was the sense that ideal golf was always within our reach, if not our grasp. And what about Jack Fleck getting a good feeling in his hands and beating Ben Hogan?

No, I thought. The U.S. Open of 1955 is as remote to her as World War I and the Great Depression were to me.

I thought about telling her that so much of golf was played in the brain and that to hit the ball well, she had to start thinking positively, to envision a good shot the way Bob Rotella had recommended, then trust that her muscles and nerves would execute it. She was tightening up over the ball. She needed to relax. She needed to understand that golf is not a game of perfect.

I could imagine what she'd say to that: Yeah, right.

The boy managed to chip onto the green about twenty feet from the hole.

"Nice chip," I told him.

The girl glowered. She dropped her ball about ten feet from the hole and took a swipe at it with her putter. It rolled by and stopped fifteen feet away.

We played on.

I thought about telling them of the Scots and their curious national character, a mix of Calvinism and humor, pragmatism and individualism. I thought of telling them how golf emerged from that culture and still reflects it.

That's ethnic stereotyping, they would say. Their education has been thorough on spotting and condemning stereotypes.

I thought about telling them that golf was a sport they could play for a long time, that it would permit them to dream and to strive even after they reached the advanced age of fifty.

But they couldn't think that far ahead. I could not have when I was their age.

Lecturing them about golf, I decided, would not help. They would get golf or not get it on their own. I kept my rebuttal to myself.

We played through six holes. The kids' shots got a little better, but not good enough to erase the frowns from their faces. The shadows by this time were gone; the sun was well below the trees on the western boundary of the golf course. The light and their patience were both about to run out.

I suggested that we cut from the sixth green to the eighteenth tee. Neither the boy nor the girl objected. We walked slowly, smelling the lingering fragrance of cut grass, a bit of honeysuckle growing by the fence along the eighth hole. A firefly flickered in front of us. At that moment in the evening, in the rapidly dying light, a curious thing happens. The color of the grass changes subtly, to a glowing shade of yellowish green. The girl's face softened some more.

"Even bad golf is good," I said, and neither of them disagreed.

We stepped onto the tee. The eighteenth is a long par four

that turns slightly from left to right. The ground falls gradually for the first three hundred yards, then turns upward for the next hundred or so to the clubhouse. The clubhouse stood before us, bulky and white in the distance. Lights glowed in the dining room. Beyond it, almost hidden, was a church across the road.

"Aim for the steeple," I suggested.

The boy set his ball on the tee and lined himself up. He was aimed, I could see, toward the trees on the left side of the fairway, trying to compensate in advance for the push-slice he'd been hitting that evening.

He took the club back slowly and swung. There was a solid click as the clubhead met the ball. It took off into the gloaming down the center of the fairway. It had the strong, boring trajectory of the well-struck wood shot. It turned slightly from right to left and then dipped below the slope of the ground, well over two hundred yards away. It rolled some more.

The boy turned, his face split with a smile.

"Nice shot," his sister said.

He just nodded, stepped away from the tee, and slid the club smoothly back into the bag.

He got it. For a moment, at least, he got it.

The essential pleasure of golf is the shot that comes off like that one did, just where he'd wanted it to go. Never mind that a swing teacher would say he accomplished it by a fortuitous accident, by combining a mistaken alignment with a mistaken swing. He accomplished it.

I don't think this pleasure ever fades. I recall once interviewing Brad Faxon for a story about an upcoming Ryder Cup match. Faxon, always seeking to use his time efficiently, likes to do such interviews during his pro-am rounds. He answers a question between a green and a tee, hits his shot, walks to the white tee to encourage his amateur partners, then answers another question during the walk to his tee shot. We were on the thirteenth tee at the Westchester Country Club. Faxon described the shot he wanted to hit—a three-wood that would travel maybe two hundred and forty yards to the end of a truncated fairway, leaving a short pitch to an elevated green. He swung. The shot took off exactly as he'd planned it. Faxon turned to me with a tight, proud little smile.

"Like *that*," he said.

It was probably only one of a million three-woods he has striped, struck in a meaningless pro-am. It didn't matter. He still loved hitting a golf ball like *that*.

So did my son. We walked off the tee toward our pleasantly distant, only dimly visible golf balls and the clubhouse beyond. I managed to refrain from commenting on the Ziegarnik Effect and how it added to the pleasure of playing the final hole, of completing a round.

Haultain, obviously, had been right. The secret of golf's attraction is not one thing but many. And somehow the whole of those discrete pleasures becomes greater than the sum of the parts. I put the thought aside. We still had approach shots to hit and a couple of putts. Three more chances, at least, to hit a ball like *that*.

Acknowledgments

I am blessed with many people to thank.

First of all, there are the people whose names are mentioned in this book as golf companions and sources of wisdom and information. I am grateful to all of them, but particularly to Bob Rotella, without whom I would never have published a word about golf or broken 80.

Then there are the magazine editors whose assignments helped me hit the road to some of the places and people explored in this book—Dave Barrett, Guy Yocom, Bob Poole, Ollie Payne, and Ken Bowden. Thanks, gentlemen.

Thanks as well to Gene Pentimonti for the scouting trip to Cullen and to Ian Findlay for his help while I was there.

Then there are the folks who read early drafts and helped me improve them—Mike Kitay, Steve Smith, Vince Desiderio, Don Tobin, and Lin Steinko.

Rafe Sagalyn, my literary agent, provided irreplaceable support and encouragement when this project was only an eccentric idea. Thanks, Rafe.

Dominick Anfuso of Simon & Schuster has been a model editor, and I am grateful to him.

Finally, my family, Ann, Peter, and Catherine, provided editorial advice, love, and encouragement. Thanks to them.

About the Author

B OB CULLEN is an award-winning journalist and critically acclaimed novelist whose work has appeared in *Newsweek, The New Yorker,* and the *Atlantic Monthly.* He collaborated with Dr. Bob Rotella on four books, beginning with the bestselling *Golf Is Not a Game of Perfect.* He lives with his wife and children in Chevy Chase, Maryland.